COVENANT THEOLOGY: A PRIMER, 2ND EDITION
by JJ Lim

© 2019 by
JJ Lim and Pilgrim Covenant Church
All rights reserved.

First published 2016 by Gratia Dei Sola Media.

Second edition, published 2019
by Pilgrim Covenant Church, Singapore
Blk 203B, Henderson Road, #07-07, Singapore 159546.
Website: www.pilgrim-covenant.com
Email: jjlim.pcc@gmail.com

Unless otherwise stated,
all Scripture quotations are from The Holy Bible:
King James Version

CONTENT

Preface

This book was never meant to be. It came about because the secretary of Gratia Dei Sola Media (GDS), sister Ming, was translating a book into Mandarin to publish serially on the society's website. She was happy with the book until she came to the chapter on covenant theology. The author has a distinctive view of covenant theology that differs from the view which the society subscribed to. The society being closely related to Pilgrim Covenant Church, Singapore, was inclined to uphold the *Westminster Standards*.

She wanted me to write a replacement chapter. But I procrastinated. It was partly because I was already overwhelmed with the ministry. But mainly it was because I did not feel competent to write on such a lofty and profound subject with the need to be succinct and yet beneficial to the average reader.

Thus, began weeks and eventually months and years of nagging by our dear sister. She reminded me of the persistent widow in our Lord's Parable! Eventually, I began to pull together paragraphs I had written elsewhere (such as in my Sabbath class notes on the *Westminster Confession of Faith*) and began stitching them together. In this way, this little booklet started to grow. Eventually Ming decided to have it published as a separate booklet by GDS. But when we had a professional proof-reader and editor go through the book, it came back in such a state that I could hardly recognise it! Sentences became disjointed (at least to me) and what appeared to be theological errors and even heretical ideas sprung up like hemlock everywhere! It was a reality check on the quality of my writing. Either the editor was trying to correct my theology or she did not understand what I was saying. Either way, it confirmed my apprehensions about the project. But Ming would not give up. Eventually, I decided that since the editor had put in so much effort to re-write my work, I must at least work on what she had produced. I spent weeks reading, re-writing and often cutting and pasting from my original document. I think I probably undid almost everything that our kind editor had done! She will probably be appalled if she finds out.

But there you have it. The first edition was eventually published; and it was translated into Mandarin and went on sale in China. Eventually, I was even invited to conduct a seminar to a group of pastors.

We had mixed reviews by English readers. Some felt they benefited from it. Others felt it was difficult to understand. Well, this second edition is an attempt to make it a little more readable and a little less technical. Whether we succeeded remains to be seen.

I am well aware that many excellent books have already been written on the subject. I am also aware that many who have studied covenant theology will differ with me on significant issues that I am presenting in this booklet. But it is my hope and prayer that this booklet will, nevertheless, be beneficial to those who are new to the subject or are keen to see an exposition of the covenant scheme adopted by the Westminster Assembly.

As this is intended to be a primer, I have not attempted to footnote most of the claims I made in it. Perhaps in future, if the Lord wills, and if there is a real need, I might enlarge on this work with proper annotations and citations. In the mean time, I will be very happy to receive any feedback on how this little work may be improved so that it may serve to exalt the name of Christ, our Covenant Head. *Soli Deo Gloria!*

—JJ Lim, March 2019

1. A BIBLICAL CONCEPT

If you have read the Bible, you have undoubtedly come across the word *covenant*. You would not read very far in the Old Testament before coming to the words of God to Noah: "I, behold, I establish my covenant with you, and with your seed after you" (Gen 9:9). In the same book, God says to Abraham: "I will establish my covenant between me and thee and thy seed after thee in their generations for an everlasting covenant, to be a God unto thee, and to thy seed after thee" (Gen 17:7). Likewise, in Deuteronomy, the last book of the Pentateuch, God says to Israel through Moses, "Know therefore that the LORD thy God, he is God, the faithful God, which keepeth covenant and mercy with them that love him and keep his commandments to a thousand generations" (Dt 7:9). Again he says in the Psalms, "The secret of the LORD is with them that fear him; and he will shew them his covenant" (Ps 25:14). In all these instances, the word "covenant" translates the Hebrew word is *berith* (בְּרִית). Indeed, the word *berith* is almost always translated as "covenant", only occasionally as "league" and once as "confederacy."

The New Testament is also replete with reference to the covenant. The Lord Jesus in establishing the Lord's Supper says, "This cup is the new testament in my blood, which is shed for you" (Lk 22:20). The Greek word translated "testament" (*diathēkē*, διαθήκη) can also be rendered "covenant." The Lord Jesus is clearly referring to the "New Covenant" spoken of by the prophet in Jeremiah 31:31. So

> **Original words:**
> - *berith*, בְּרִית :
>   covenant, league
> - *diathēkē*, διαθήκη :
>   testament, covenant

the apostle to the Hebrews tells us that "Jesus [is] the mediator of the new covenant" (Heb 12:24) and that His blood which is shed for us is "the blood of the everlasting covenant" (Heb 13:20).

It is clear then, that whatever a covenant may be, it is an important biblical concept and has implications not only for the saints in Old Testament times but also for us who are New Testament believers.

What is a covenant?

Many theologians think of covenants in terms of contracts or agreements, and they have good justification for that; for do we not read in the Scriptures of covenants between man and man, which are clearly some kinds of agreement or contract? Consider for examples, the covenant between Abraham and Abimelech, made at Beersheba (Gen 21:32); the covenant between Isaac and the later Abimelech (Gen 26:28); and the covenant between Jacob and Laban (Gen 31:44). These are clearly bilateral agreements or contracts between two parties, stating the conditions, benefits, and penalties of each. Usually, these covenants required a pledge or sign and seal. In the covenant between Abraham and Abimelech, the pledge was "seven ewe lambs" (Gen 21:30) whereas in the covenant between Jacob and Laban, it was a heap of stone (Gen 31:48). The condition was really the promise of each party. If the participants kept their promise, they would reap the benefit of the covenant, or, at least not incur the penalty for failing to honour it. In the covenant between Jacob and Laban, Laban promised to let Jacob keep his wives, children, and livestock (31:43), and not to cross the boundary stone that Jacob set up. On the other hand, Jacob promised to treat his wives well (v. 50) and not to cross the boundary line (v. 52). Each party of this covenant called upon God to exact punishment if either of them broke his promise (v. 53).

Covenant:
A relationship between two parties which is built upon mutual promises or vows.

Elements of a Covenant:
a. Parties
b. Conditions
c. Blessings
d. Curses
e. Optional Sign & Seal

The covenants in these cases appear to be no more than contracts or agreements. The parties have no real friendship with one another, but they enter into a contract to define how they should relate to one another rather than fight with one another. Such covenants may be termed 'business covenants' as depicted in Figure 1.

God as Witness

Cooperation/
Partnership

Sworn Agreement / Mutual Contract
i.e. Conditions, Benefits & Penalties

Party A

Party B

Figure 1: *A Business Covenant:*
Partnership or agreement sealed by a contract, in which
the covenant is no more than a contract

Some covenants are more than a contract. Consider the *league* or *covenant* of peace made between Israel and the Gibeonites (Jos 9:15); or the one between King Solomon and King Hiram of Tyre (1 Kgs 5:12). Israel was tricked into a covenant with Gibeon, but once the agreement was made Israel was obligated to defend her covenant partner. That was why the Gibeonites appealed to Joshua to rescue them from the five kings led by Adonizedek (cf. Jos 10:6), even though Israel's only promise was to let the Gibeonites live and dwell in peace (Jos 9:15). Conversely, the covenant between Solomon and Hiram was based on friendship between David, the father of Solomon, and Hiram (1 Kgs 5:1). That existing relationship became covenantal when Solomon and Hiram entered into an agreement. This was more than a contract, for at the heart of it was friendship between the two nations.

Such is generally the case in covenants of peace between nations. See Figure 2.

Figure 2: *A Covenant of Peace between Nations:*
in which friendship is sealed by mutual agreement

But what about God's covenant with man? It cannot be that God has made an agreement with man as if God and man were equal parties in the covenant; for God is sovereign and in control of all things whereas man is a finite creature.

Thus, some highly respected theologians, such as Meredith Kline[1] and Michael Horton[2] suggest that God's covenant with man may best be understood as being patterned after Ancient Near Eastern, Ugaritic or Hittite Royal Grants or Suzerainty Treaties.[3] Typically, in such treaties,

---

[1] See Meredith Kline, *Treaty of the Great King: The Covenant Structure of Deuteronomy: Studies and Commentary* (Grand Rapids: William B. Erdmans Publishing Company, 1963), 14ff.

[2] See Michael Horton, *Introducing Covenant Theology* (Grand Rapids: Baker Academic, 2006), 10.

[3] Covenants of Grants and Covenants of Suzerainty are often distinguished by the weight of responsibility placed upon the greater or the lesser party respectively. In that sense Grants are more benevolent, whereas Suzerainties are more self-serving for the greater party. See for example, *Peter Golding, Covenant Theology: The Key of Theology in Reformed Thought and Tradition* (Ross-shire: Christian Focus

a superior nation or king promises to bless, to protect, or at least, not to obliterate, a vassal nation upon some stated conditions such as obedience and tributes. Figure 3 illustrates such a scheme.

Figure 3: Typical Suzerainty Covenant

While it is fascinating to compare some of the covenantal passages in Scripture[4] with these pagan treaties, it appears to us to be disingenuous to interpret God's covenant, which has divine and eternal origin with them. Surely God did not imitate man, whereas man could well have imitated and perverted God's designs.

Indeed, further examination of the Scripture reveals that God's covenant with man may, at some level, be understood as unilateral and unconditional for man. Genesis 15 explains how God cut a covenant with Abraham (v. 18). This was validated according to the ancient Near-Eastern customs of covenant-making,[5] in which several

---

Publications, 2004), 69-70). In practice, however, the Fall of man ensures that there is no unconditional benevolence amongst men.

[4] Eg. Exodus 19-24; Deuteronomy; and Joshua 24.

[5] It is a moot point whether the original practice came about through God's instruction or simply through the invention of man; but whatever the case may be, it

animals were cut in half and laid out so both parties of the covenant could walk between the pieces while calling a curse upon themselves if they failed to keep their promise (cf. Jer 34:18). Abraham did not pass through the pieces; he was fast asleep though he was made aware of what was going on (v. 12). What passed through the pieces was clearly a theophany (v. 17).

With this in mind, some theologians insist that we should not speak of divine covenants as contracts or agreements, and that we should not speak of God's covenant with man as having any conditions at all. They prefer to speak of such covenants as bonds of love or friendship. There is good biblical basis for saying that, for the covenant that God made with Abraham is clearly a demonstration of unconditional love.

The problem is that in the Bible the same word is used to describe the covenant between man and man as well as a covenant between God and man.[6] God wants us to understand that the concept of a divine covenant cannot be distinguished entirely from covenants between men. More specifically, it appears that the conditions and agreement cannot be eviscerated from biblical covenants. Indeed, even the covenant that God made with Abraham suggests conditions and agreement, at least on God's part.

---

was apparently commonly practised by the time of Abraham and it was approved by the LORD.

[6] To this assertion, it is objected that the New Testament translates בְּרִית with διαθήκη (which is often translated in the English New Testament as "Testament" i.e. "will", eg. Heb 9:16-17), rather than συνθήκη (which clearly carries the idea of a bi-lateral compact), many commentators insist that God's Covenant with man must never be viewed as conditional bilateral, but as unconditional and unilateral. But the problem is that συνθήκη occurs very rarely in the LXX (Dan 11:6; Isa 28:15; 30:1; and apocrypha: Wis 1:16; 1 Mac 10:26) and is used to translate בְּרִית only once; whereas διαθήκη is also used to translate בְּרִית when it refers to conditional, bilateral covenants between man and man (eg. Gen 21:27, 32; 26:28; 31:44 etc). Thus διαθήκη does not necessarily imply unilateral unconditional covenant.

Thus, biblical data teaches that God's covenant with us is conditional from one perspective and unconditional from another. It also leads us to the idea that God's covenant relationship with His children is one of unconditional love, although the relationship is undergirded by a covenantal agreement. This concept is all very vague at the moment, but I believe it will become clearer as we look at the specifics of God's covenantal relationship with us.

But for now, it may help to think of divine covenants in terms of marriage (cf. Mal 2:14) rather than a business contract or suzerainty treaties. Marriage is a bond of love rather than a mere contract; yet it differs from courtship because it is sealed by mutual vows. In marriage, there are two parties. There is a set of conditions for the husband and another set for the wife. There are blessings for fulfilling the conditions, such as marital bliss, mutual benefits, children, etc. There are also implied curses or penalties associated with breaking the conditions, such as marital torments, loss of privileges, suits, etc. See Figure 4.

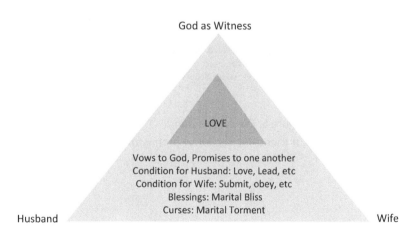

Figure 4: *A Marriage Covenant:*
In which love is sealed by solemn vows

God's covenant with man is like that: it is a bond of friendship or love sealed by promissory oaths. Like marriage, the two parties vow to keep their respective promises that undergird the relationship. But unlike marriage, the two parties are not equals, for God is infinitely greater than man. Thus, divine covenants must be

> **Divine Covenant:**
> *A bond of friendship or love between God and man which is sealed by promisory oaths and sovereignly administered.*

sovereignly administered. God determines the terms and condescends to bless; whereas man must acquiesce and obey if he is to enjoy the covenantal relationship with God. See Figure 5.

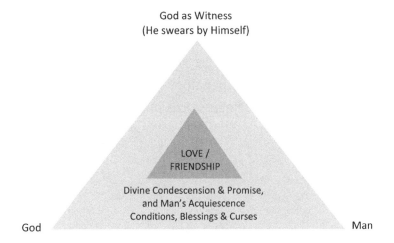

Figure 5: *Divine Covenant:*
A bond of love or friendship sealed by promissory oaths

2. A RELATIONAL FRAMEWORK

A covenant is an important biblical concept that may be defined as a bond of relationship sealed by promissory oaths. This relationship is one of friendship or love in the covenant between God and man. Therefore, we may define God's covenant with us as a bond of friendship or love sealed by promissory oaths. Those who are truly in an unbroken covenant relationship with God enjoy a bond of mutual love with God.

It is important for us to distinguish between an oath and a covenant. An oath is part of a covenant, but the covenant is more than an oath; just as the marriage vow is part of marriage but marriage is more than the vow. Thus, Scripture makes a distinction between a covenant and the oath of the covenant. For example, in Ezekiel 16:59, God condemns His people for despising His oath and breaking the covenant.

Again, while the covenant is closely related to the relationship between parties, it is not the relationship itself but a framework for enjoying the relationship. Think of marriage again. At the heart of an ideal marriage is a relationship between a husband and wife. This relationship can be described as unconditional love. But this love can only be enjoyed within a covenantal framework. The covenant, then, may be spoken of as a means to an end, yet the covenant must not be sharply distinguished from the end, for to do so would rob it of its warmth and purpose.

It is not helpful, either, to define covenant simply as "an agreement upon an oath" because that makes the covenant a cold mechanical means; whereas the covenant itself is not only a means to initiate and facilitate the relationship but also part of enjoying the relationship. Thus, Scripture refers to a new covenant (Jer 31:31) although nothing pertaining to the covenant framework has changed between the old and new covenant. The parties, the condition, the blessings and the curses remain the same. The only thing that changes is the administration of the covenant or the enjoyment of the covenant relationship by God's people.

This is all rather complicated. But again, it is important for us to bear these things in mind as we consider the question: "Why covenant?" or more specifically, "Why is there a need for covenant in the context of our relationship with God?"

Some say there is no real need other than that God is a covenantal God, and the Persons of the Godhead are forever in a covenant bond of love; and therefore, God relates with His elect with the same covenant bond. The problem with this view is that it has very little biblical justification. Scripture does allude to a covenant between the Father and the Son (eg. Ps 2:7–9; Ps 40:7–9; Jn 6:38–39; 17:5, 6, 9, 24), but the covenant relationship is economic

> **Ontological:**
> Pertaining to the nature of God
>
> **Economic:**
> Pertaining to God's external work
>
> **Redemptive:**
> Pertaining to God's plan of salvation for man
>
> **Pantheistic:**
> The idea that reality is identical to, or is an extension of God's nature.

and redemptive rather than ontological. The idea that the essence of the covenant must be derived or explained from the ontological relationship between the Persons of the Trinity seems to be more pantheistic than biblical. Also, this idea must necessarily lead to a rejection of the element of agreement or conditional promises that are implied in the biblical references to covenants, at least in the Old Testament. When this element is removed, *covenant* ceases to be a covenant in the biblical sense of the word. What remains is really the relationship of love.

Perhaps a better way of looking at the necessity of the covenant is to see it as the framework God has chosen to enable finite men to understand and enjoy their relationship with God. The *Westminster Confession of Faith* alludes to this idea by stating:

> WCF 7.1: *The distance between God and the creature is so great, that although reasonable creatures do owe obedience unto Him as their Creator, yet they could never have any fruition of Him as their blessedness and reward, but by some voluntary condescension on God's part, which He hath been pleased to express by way of covenant*
>
> Isa 40:13–17; Job 9:32–33; 1 Sam 2:25; Ps 113:5–6; 100:2–3; Job 22:2–3; 35:7–8; Lk 17:10; Acts 17:24–25.

The distance between God as Creator and man as creature is frequently emphasized in Scripture. Because man's existence is dependent on God, man owes God absolute obedience and, therefore, cannot expect to be rewarded for it. It is to illustrate this point that our Lord told His disciples that a master does not thank his slave for doing his duties (Lk 17:10). God has, nevertheless, condescended to relate to us in a way that allows us to enjoy Him and to receive His blessings upon our obedience. Scripture suggests that the means or the relationship framework that God has chosen for this purpose is the covenant. Thus, the *Confession* speaks of how God has condescended to relate to men by way of covenant so that they may have some "fruition [or enjoyment] of Him as their blessedness and reward."

It is important to remember that the concept of covenant is a creation of God. We must not think that God adopted a human practice to relate to man: for God's covenant to redeem man from sin was in place even before man was created. Thus, it must be that man makes covenants because God originated the idea and led man to see it and use it in his relationship with one another.

3. FIRST INSTANCE

The *Westminster Confession of Faith*, having explained the necessity of the covenant as a relational framework to bridge the distance between infinite God and finite man, proceeds immediately to show us how it actually works out:

> *WCF 7.2—The first covenant made with man was a Covenant of Works, wherein life was promised to Adam; and in him to his posterity upon condition of perfect and personal obedience.*
>
> *Gal 3:12; Rom 10:5; 5:12–20; Gen 2:17; Gal 3:10.*

The first man, Adam, was the appointed representative of man. As God entered into a relationship with man so that man might enjoy Him, He made a covenant with Adam. God would deal with Adam as the head of the federation of mankind. Adam's role in the covenant would be like the role of a king in entering into a covenant relationship with another nation. If the king breaks the covenant, every citizen of his nation breaks the covenant. If the king declares war, every citizen in his nation is at war.

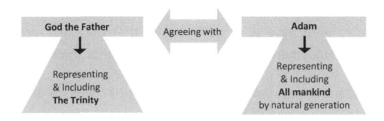

Figure 6: The Parties in the Covenant of Works

The covenant that God made with Adam is known as the Covenant of Works, or the Covenant of Life. It is called the Covenant of Life because the blessing of the covenant was life, whereas its penalty was death. It is called the Covenant of Works because the condition stipulated by God for man to enjoy life is perfect and personal obedience, or in other words, an impeccable observance of God's Law.

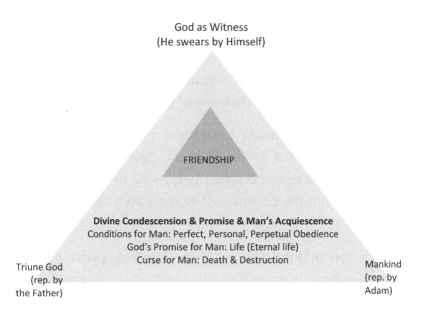

Figure 7: *Covenant of Works:*
A bond of friendship sealed by promissory oaths
(With conditions utterly broken by Adam)

By nature, man is bounded to obey his Creator. God owes him nothing for his obedience. However, God, in entering into a covenant with man, condescends to reward man with life if he obeys God perfectly.

In the administration of the covenant, God instructed Adam not to eat of a special tree in the Garden of Eden known as the Tree of the Knowledge of Good and Evil. We are not told much about this tree. In all likelihood, it was an ordinary tree: for its fruit was good for food (Gen 3:6), at least for the animals. However, God told Adam: "Thou shalt not eat of it: for in the day that thou eatest thereof thou shalt surely die" (Gen 2:17). This was a test of obedience for Adam. Adam must not eat of the tree not because the fruit could be poisonous, but because God forbade him from doing so. If he ate from the tree, he would violate the condition of the covenant and die.

As it turns out, Adam ate the forbidden fruit. Thus, he broke the covenant, and all his descendants by ordinary generation became covenant-breakers and are liable for the penalty of the covenant. God never revoked the Covenant of Works, but we can never again have life by the Covenant of Works because we are by nature guilty in Adam. We are saved today not through the Covenant of Works, but through Christ's work as the Mediator of the Covenant of Grace.

We will look at the Covenant of Grace in more detail later, but for now, let us focus on the necessity of the Covenant of Works, for it provides the answer to some rather perplexing passages in Scripture. And not only so, but the Covenant of Grace is built upon the Covenant of Works!

Some may object that the word *covenant* does not appear in Genesis 1 to 3 and, therefore, it is unbiblical to speak of a Covenant of Works. However, there are three good reasons to believe that God did make a covenant with Adam:

First, the Hebrew of Hosea 6:7 is better rendered: "They like *Adam* have transgressed the covenant" rather than "They like *men* have transgressed the covenant." We say this, in the first place, because the Hebrew *adam* is singular. And in the second place, if Israel did not transgress the covenant "like men," how else would they have transgressed it, since they are men? The same Hebrew word translated "like men" (כְּאָדָם, *ke-adam*) is translated "as Adam" in Job 31:33, —"If I covered my transgressions as Adam, by hiding mine iniquity in my bosom."

> **Biblical Evidence for the Covenant of Works:**
>
> - *Reference to Adam breaking the covenant in Hosea 6:7*
> - *Comparision between Christ and Adam in Romans 5:12-21*
> - *Jesus' teaching that eternal life may be obtained by perfect observance of the Law*

Second, the apostle Paul offers a clear parallel between Adam and Christ in Romans 5:12–21 in connection with the doctrine of justification. This parallel can only make sense if Adam, like Christ, is the head of a covenant. Just as Adam's sin was imputed to his posterity whom he represented, Christ's righteousness is imputed to the elect whom He represents.

Third, the gospels include a couple of occasions when the Lord Jesus is asked: "What shall I do that I may inherit eternal life?" (Mk 10:17; cf. Mt 19:16; Lk 18:18; see also Lk 10:25). In each instance, the Lord's answer is, essentially, to keep the law perfectly. Is the Lord wrong or deceitful in His answer? Of course not! But surely, He is not suggesting that law-keeping or good works can *merit* eternal life. Even in man's unfallen state in the Garden of Eden, obedience was his expected duty, not something that merited anything (Lk 17:10). The fact is: if there were no Covenant of Works, obedience could not obtain eternal life! So our Lord's answer only makes sense if there is indeed a Covenant of Works, which has not been abrogated. If there were no Covenant of Works or if it was abrogated, then the Lord's answer would be erroneous or deceitful, which would contradict His divine nature. The inquirers had asked what they could *do* to obtain eternal life. The Lord honestly answered that the only way of obtaining life *by doing* is through perfect obedience of God's law under the provision of the Covenant of Works! Of course, fallen man cannot keep the Covenant of Works. Fallen man may only obtain life by faith in the One who kept the Covenant of Works, even Jesus!

It is fascinating to see how the Lord steered the rich young ruler (Mk 10:17) away from himself, by showing him that while he might theoretically obtain life by keeping the law, he could not, for he could not even keep the 10th commandment, seeing that he would not obey the instruction, of one he had just acknowledged as God, to sell everything he had. Did he eventually understand what the Lord was teaching and placed his faith entirely upon Him? Was this rich young man actually Joseph of Arimathea, who showed gratitude to the Lord for leading him to life everlasting by turning him away from self-righteousness? Perhaps; for does not Mark 10:21 testify that Jesus loved him?

4. THE COVENANT OF WORKS

The first covenant that God made with man was the Covenant of Works. The *Westminster Shorter Catechism* refers to this covenant as the Covenant of Life in the answer to question 12:

> *"When God had created man, He entered into a covenant of life with him—upon condition of perfect obedience—forbidding him to eat of the tree of the knowledge of good and evil, upon the pain of death."*

Although this covenant is not explicitly named the Covenant of Works in Scripture, its existence is clearly implied and may easily be inferred from various Scripture texts. We have already seen this in chapter 3. But now let us look at the covenant; this time in a more systematic way.

We noted that a covenant has four essential elements: (1) The Parties; (2) The Condition or Stipulation; (3) The Blessing or Benefits; and (4) The Curses or Penalty. We also noted that usually there is also an accompanying pledge or sign.

The Parties of the Covenant

The parties in the Covenant of Works are God on the one hand, and man on the other. More specifically, the two parties are the Triune God as represented by the Father, and Man represented by Adam. Note that God is the Creator, whereas man is His creature. Naturally, the creature is duty-bound to keep the laws of the Creator, and as such his obedience merits nothing, though disobedience deserves punishment. But God, having entered into a covenant with man, has graciously taken upon Himself to reward man for keeping the condition of the covenant and to punish him for failure to fulfil the condition. In other words, God has condescended to deal with man not according to nature but according to the covenant framework that He places him in.

The Condition

The condition of the Covenant of Works, as we have seen, is perfect, personal obedience to the moral law of God. Adam had the moral law written in his heart since He was created in the image of God. Thus, Paul says:

> "For when the Gentiles, which have not the law, do by nature the things contained in the law, these, having not the law, are a law unto themselves: Which shew the work of the law written in their hearts, their conscience also bearing witness, and their thoughts the mean while accusing or else excusing one another" (Rom 2:14–15).

The moral law of God is summarized in the Ten Commandments, but in a different form. The Ten Commandments in Exodus 20 are predominantly negative because they presuppose knowledge of sin. But Adam knew no sin, so the law inscribed on his heart must have been positive. Moreover, since he knew no sin, he would have found it natural, effortless, and reasonable to obey the moral law. So God deemed it necessary to add a negative commandment that was, in some sense, arbitrary and indifferent. He said to Adam: "But of the tree of the knowledge of good and evil, thou shalt not eat of it: for in the day that thou eatest thereof thou shalt surely die" (Gen 2:17).

Adam must not eat of the forbidden tree for no other reason than God told him not to do so. It was a test of pure obedience. Would Adam obey God, or would he follow the guidance of his own judgement? In that sense, the demands of the law were concentrated on one point: if Adam obeyed, he and his posterity would receive the blessings of the covenant, but if he failed, he and his posterity would experience the curses.

The Blessing

We noted that the blessing of the Covenant of Works is life. This is why it is sometimes called the Covenant of Life. But what kind of life is it?

Some, especially those who do not believe in a Covenant of Works, would insist that Adam was not promised life but threatened with death if he disobeyed God. For them, the life that Adam could have was only a continuation of natural earthly life. Similarly, others assert that eternal life could only come through the Lord Jesus Christ; therefore, even if Adam were promised life, it would only be a happy earthly existence.

But comparing Scripture with Scripture, we are compelled to say that eternal life was indeed promised to Adam. Did not the Lord Jesus say to people who asked what they should do to inherit eternal life that they must obey the commandments (e.g. Mk 10:17; Lk 10:25; 18:18)? No doubt our Lord had in mind the Covenant of Works.

> *The Covenant of Works:*
> - *Parties:*
>   God and Man represented by Adam
> - *Condition:*
>   Perfect, personal and perpetual obedience by man
> - *Blessing:*
>   Life, even Eternal life
> - *Curses:*
>   Death, even bodily, spiritual and eternal death
> - *Pledge or Sign & Seal:*
>   The Tree of Life

Now, the *quality* of eternal life that could be obtained by Adam's obedience could not possibly have been nearly as complete as what is obtained by Christ's obedience, for Adam was created as a man whereas Christ is the God-Man. But we have scriptural warrant to speak of the benefit of the Covenant of Works as being eternal life. In a sense, Adam was already enjoying a degree of eternal life before the Fall, for eternal life according to the Lord Jesus is a life of knowing and enjoying God. That is what He is essentially saying in His high priestly prayer: "This is life eternal, that they might know thee the only true God, and Jesus Christ, whom thou hast sent" (Jn 17:3).

Of course, Adam could lose that life by sinning, so his quality of life could not be eternal or everlasting. Nevertheless, we have reason to believe that if he stood the test of obedience, he would have been lifted to a higher plane after an indefinite period. The biblical basis of this assertion is how the good angels were confirmed in righteousness. If Adam had obeyed God, he would have been raised above the possibility of sinning and dying. That is the implicit promise. That also helps us understand numerous passages in Scripture that speak of obtaining life through good works or by keeping God's law, such as the following:

- Romans 7:10: *And the commandment, which was ordained to life, I found to be unto death*. i.e., "The law was designed and adapted to secure life, but became in fact the cause of death" (Charles Hodge).

- Romans 10:5: *For Moses describeth the righteousness which is of the law, That the man which doeth those things shall live by them.*

- Leviticus 18:5: *Ye shall therefore keep my statutes, and my judgments: which if a man do, he shall live in them: I am the* LORD.

- Galatians 3:12: And *the law is not of faith: but, The man that doeth them shall live in them.*

- Ezekiel 20:11: *And I gave them my statutes, and shewed them my judgments, which if a man do, he shall even live in them* (cf. Ezk 20:13, 21).

The Curses

The curses of the Covenant of Works are also clearly stated by the LORD to Adam: "But of the tree of the knowledge of good and evil, thou shalt not eat of it: for in the day that thou eatest thereof *thou shalt surely die*" (Gen 2:17).

The intensity of the words in Hebrew (תָּמֻת מוֹת, *tamuth moth*, lit.: "dying, ye shall die") suggests that more than physical death is involved. Comparing Scripture with Scripture, we may conclude that three levels of death are involved: physical, spiritual, and eternal (cf. *WCF* 6.6).

- *Physical death* refers to bodily degradation and demise. The minute Adam violated the covenant, his body, in a sense, died, for he could no longer glorify or enjoy God with his body. And moreover, he became mortal. He began the process of bodily decay which would eventually lead to death. The Lord pronounced after Adam fell: "In the sweat of thy face shalt thou eat bread, *till thou return unto the ground; for out of it wast thou taken: for dust thou art, and unto dust shalt thou return*" (Gen 3:19). Physical death is one evil that Christ came to reverse. As Paul says to the Corinthians, "But now is Christ risen from the dead, and become the firstfruits of them that slept. For since by man came death, by man came also the resurrection of the dead. *For as in Adam all die*, even so in Christ shall all be made alive" (1 Cor 15:20–22).

- *Spiritual death* refers to deadness in the soul, making a person totally unable to do good in the sight of God or to glorify and enjoy God. When Adam fell, he and his posterity became "dead in trespasses and sin" (Eph 2:1), and all their righteousness were as "filthy rags" (Isa 64:6) in the eyes of God. Christ, the Second Adam, was sent to reverse the effects of spiritual death for His people. Thus Paul says: "For if by one man's offence death reigned by one; much more they which receive abundance of grace and of the gift of righteousness shall reign in life by one, Jesus Christ" (Rom 5:17).

- *Eternal death* refers to the permanent inability to enjoy God's fellowship and love in this life, which inevitably culminates at bodily death, to suffering the full wrath of God forever and ever. Eternal death is symbolized in Genesis 3:24 when the Lord drives Adam out of the Garden of Eden: "So he drove out the man; and he placed at the east of the garden of Eden cherubims, and a flaming sword which turned every way, to keep the way of the tree of life." Christ came to undo eternal death and replace it with eternal life for His people: "For the wages of sin is *death*; but the gift of God is *eternal life* through Jesus Christ our Lord" (Rom 6:23).

The Pledge or Sign and Seal

Although the sign and seal is an optional element in a covenant, it is instructive for us for to see how God appointed a pledge to the Covenant of Works just as He would appoint two for the Covenant of Grace, which we will consider shortly. The pledge of the Covenant of Works is the Tree of Life (*WLC* 20). As the esteemed Reformed theologian Francis Turretin writes:

[The Tree of Life] was a sacrament and symbol of the immortality which would have been bestowed upon Adam if he had persevered in his first state. Augustine says, "He had nourishment in other trees; in this, however, a sacrament." Now this signification can have a threefold relation. (1) With respect to past life, it was a symbol putting him in mind of the life received from God. As often as he tasted its fruit, he was bound to recollect that he had life not from himself, but from God. (2) With respect to future life, it was a declarative and sealing sign of the happy life to be passed in paradise and to be changed afterwards into a heavenly life, if he had continued upright. (3) With respect to the state of grace, it was an illustrious type of the eternal happiness prepared for us in heaven; also a type of Christ himself who acquired and confers it upon us and who is therefore called "the tree of life in the midst of the paradise of God" (Rev 2:7); "the tree of life yielding her fruit twelve times every month, whose leaves are for the healing of the nations" (Rev 22:2).[7]

Conclusion

When we use Scripture to interpret Scripture many theological points which appear to be contradictory are proven not to be. A theological proposition can easily be dismissed as fallacious if there are only one or two isolated verses in Scriptures to support it. But if it is found to be tightly interconnected with other established propositions, or if it includes satisfying and consistent elaboration in other parts of Scripture, then it must not be quickly dismissed despite the objections of reputable theologians. Let us rather, "Prove all things; hold fast that which is good" (1 Th 5:21).

The doctrine of the Covenant of Works is a biblical idea worthy of acceptance. Not only does it provide a consistent framework for the interpretation of numerous portions of Scripture which are otherwise difficult to understand, but it also forms the basis of the Covenant of Grace, which we shall see in the next chapter.

---

[7] Francis Turretin, *Institutes of Elenctic Theology*, 8.5.3 (vol 1, p. 581).

5. A BEAUTIFUL STEPPING STONE

It is clear that the Covenant of Works is implied in Scripture. We have considered its elements. But what is the significance of this covenant? How is it relevant to us? Let me suggest three applications to answer these questions using the three words: *love, wisdom*, and *grace*.

Love

First, the covenant of life indirectly shows us that God's relationship with man is one of love. True religion is defined by love. False religions are defined by idolatry and legalism.

The Covenant of Life is not merely a contract. It is rather a means for us to enjoy God's fellowship. It demonstrates how God intends for man to enjoy fellowship with Him. When we enjoy a relationship with someone, we derive pleasure from giving to and receiving from that person. If we give and receive nothing, we miss out on enjoyment, particularly in the relationship. We find joy when we give and then receive, or when we receive and give, and continue doing so.

But man is a creature of dust. How could we enjoy fellowship with the almighty God? Why should God give in response to our giving? He owes us nothing. Perhaps that is why God entered into a covenant relationship with us, in which He condescends to receive from and to give to us, poor creatures of dust, so that we may know we are not insignificant in His eyes. The Covenant of Life assures us that God is not unmoved when we love Him and serve Him, for God promises to bless us richly when we keep His covenant.

Today man is fallen and can no longer obtain eternal life by the Covenant of Life. But Christ has perfectly fulfilled the Covenant of Life so that we who are represented by Christ are enabled to enjoy a relationship with God under the terms of the Covenant of Grace. The principles of the Covenant of Life were never abolished, for God is still pleased to bless those who would walk in obedience to His commandments by His grace.

Indeed, the Covenant of Life suggests to us that friendship with God must be according to His terms. Loving God is obeying God. We cannot say we love God and then do what we want without regard to God's will. We can do a lot of things for God, but if we fail to do what God commands, then we fail to love God. Adam failed to love God because he ate the forbidden fruit when God specifically told him not to eat it. But those who are in Christ have the image of God restored in them and are enabled to love the Lord by His Spirit working in their heart.

Indeed, those in Christ are bonded together under a new covenant and a new covenant head. We no longer belong to the old Covenant of Life and to the world which is united under the Covenant of Life. We belong rather to Christ and are bonded together with Him and with one another in a family of love, peace, and hope. The greatest of these is love, Scripture says. The Covenant of Life reminds us that it is God's will that we walk in love and enjoy love.

Wisdom

Second, if you think about it carefully, you will see that the Covenant of Life is a wonderful display of God's wisdom. The Covenant of Life is not an end in itself; it is rather a means to an end. When you understand God's plan of salvation, you realize that God never intended for the elect to obtain eternal life through Adam's obedience. Christ was always in the plan of salvation. He was never a secondary option.

God in His wisdom set the Covenant of Life in place, first, as a stepping stone to the Covenant of Grace, and second, to demonstrate the fairness and wisdom of God.

Man was made with the ability to choose to retain and sustain life under the Covenant of Life, but he forfeited that opportunity by sinning against God. God sent His Son to save His elect, but not by giving Him special treatment. Christ was the second Adam and would be tried as Adam was tried, only more severely. He would gain for His elect what Adam lost. All praise be to Him! If you think about it, you realize that this plan could not be invented by men. Its totality is revealed in Scripture in a number of seemingly unrelated passages and yet can be put together so systematically that we can only pause to consider its origin. It cannot be a mere human invention, for the mode of revelation and its marvellous consistency bears the fingerprints of divine design. Praise the Lord!

Grace

Third, the Covenant of Life provides us with a vivid demonstration of God's grace. God's eternal plan is that a multitude of sons and daughters share His image to enjoy fellowship with Him for all eternity with a personal knowledge of the fullness of His mercy and justice. God could have created us in an instant the way that He created angels. He could also have made us infallibly righteous. But He preferred to have us know Him as a just God who is full of mercy and grace. This is why He created man with the capacity to disobey. That is also why He ordained the Covenant of Life, for it helps man realize that he cannot obtain life by himself even though God promises to reward him with life if he chooses to love and obey Him. The covenant provided the way to have life, but man forfeited the right. Man deserves to be cast away forever, yet God graciously brought man to Himself.

Though God's friendship with mankind was broken because of Adam's sin, God provided a way for man to again enjoy friendship with him. That is through the Lord Jesus Christ, who came as the second Adam. He would do what Adam failed to do: keep God's laws perfectly. And He would die to pay the penalty of our sin in Adam.

How costly it was to redeem man! But God did not shirk from it. He set up the Covenant of Life for man's sake. Now that the Covenant of Life is in place, God provides life through it by the Son of God. We deserve to be cast away not only for disobeying God, but also for despising God's goodness and love. Yet, wonder of wonders, God instead of casting us away, paid a great price to redeem us that we might enjoy eternity with Him. Oh how we must love Him and serve Him with gratitude!

All who believe in the Lord Jesus Christ can enjoy exceedingly more deeply the friendship of God that Adam enjoyed in the Garden of Eden. In fact, all who would believe in Christ would have been beloved in Christ before the foundation of the world (Eph 1:4), and therefore, they would enjoy not merely friendship, but infinite love in Christ!

6. THE SECOND INSTANCE

The Covenant of Works was the first instance of God's covenant relationship with man. Therein, God graciously covenanted to reward Adam and his posterity with life upon condition of perfect obedience. But Adam fell into sin, and with him, all mankind descending from him by ordinary generation could no longer obtain life by the first covenant.

The Covenant of Grace is God's gracious provision for fallen man to enjoy life. This covenant is not an afterthought which God instituted only after the Covenant of Works failed. The Covenant of Grace had always been in God's mind. It logically precedes the Covenant of Works even though the Covenant of Works was manifested first. This is a bit hard to explain. But think of the Covenant of Works as a stepping stone to the Covenant of Grace, just as the Fall was a stepping stone for us to enjoy God in Christ.

The Covenant of Grace is referred to in numerous places in Scripture, but Genesis 15 provides us with, perhaps, the most complete and beautiful picture of it. This chapter actually contains two great doctrines: the doctrine of justification by grace through faith and the doctrine of the Covenant of Grace. The doctrine of justification is taught in the first six verses of the chapter. From there we see how God encouraged Abram after rescuing Lot by telling him that He was Abram's shield and exceeding great reward. Abram, no doubt, understood the Lord to be reiterating His twin promises to him.

The first promise was that God would bless Abram with many children. But we must understand that this is not merely about his having many descendants. Ultimately it refers to the birth of his Descendant Christ Jesus and a multitude of people who would be united to him in Christ. Abram would be a blessing to the world through Christ.

The second promise is that Abram would inherit the Promised Land. But again this was not merely a promise about the land. Ultimately it refers to the eternal inheritance in heaven for all those who are united to Christ. These two promises are yea and amen in Christ. They are meaningless apart from Christ. They would, however, be fulfilled typically in Abram having many children and in his children inheriting the land of Canaan.

To reiterate that He would keep His promises, God directed Abram to look up to the night sky at the stars, which were too numerous to count. As he did so, God assured him that his seed would be as innumerable as the stars in the sky. Abram believed God, and it was counted unto him for righteousness. He believed the promises of God, which would be completely fulfilled in the Messiah. Abram was justified by grace through faith as are all who are the true children of Abram in Christ.

But God was not done assuring Abram that He would keep His promises. He tells Abram in verse 7: "I am the LORD that brought thee out of Ur of the Chaldees, to give thee this land to inherit it." Abram, as he did before, sought further assurance and clarification. The land was still in the hands of the Canaanites, so how would God fulfil His promise to give this land to the descendants of Abram? Abram asks the Lord in verse 8, "LORD GOD, whereby shall I know that I shall inherit it?" God's response was that Abram should prepare a contract to seal a covenant.

We have already seen that a covenant is a bond of relationship that is governed by an agreement between two parties. It is like a contract, but it is more than that for it involves a relationship that transcends the contract. A covenant has basically four elements: (1) two parties enjoying a bond of friendship; (2) conditions or promises by both parties; (3) curses for breaking the promises; and (4) blessings for keeping the promises.

We noted that one example of a covenant in human life is marriage. In marriage, there is friendship between the husband and wife; but they are more than friends. They have vowed to love one another exclusively. If they keep their promises to one another, they will enjoy many blessings: love, security, children, joy, and family. But if they break their promises, they will suffer the pains and sorrows associated with a broken marriage.

If two people are just friends, they may part company if they discover that they don't like one another. They have no obligations towards each other apart from emotional obligations. But if they are married, they cannot just part company without suffering painful consequences.

Think of the marriage certificate as a contract, but the relationship of love when it is sealed by the vows (which are captured in the contract) as a covenant. Without the vows, the relationship would not be a covenant. Without the relationship of love, the vows would be hypocritical and the contract would be empty and mechanical. That would make a sham of marriage and reduce the covenant vows to no more than a business contract.

God instructed Abram to prepare a contract to seal the relationship between the two. In those days, a contract was not simply a piece of paper which the parties sign. It was much more. Let us examine that contract under three headings: (1) Preparation for the Contract; (2) Parties in the Covenant; (3) Promises of the Covenant.

Preparation for the Contract

God instructed Abram to prepare the contract. He said in Genesis 15:9–10:

"Take me an heifer of three years old, and a she goat of three years old, and a ram of three years old, and a turtledove, and a young

pigeon. And he took unto him all these, and divided them in the midst, and laid each piece one against another: but the birds divided he not."

Abram was to take these birds and animals and kill them, cutting them in two. Then he was to line up these bloody parts to form a path between them. Half of the heifer would be on the left and half on the right. Half of the goat and ram would be on the left and the other half on the right. Only the birds were not divided.

What was Abram doing? Abram was preparing a contract! In those days when two parties would make a contract, they would get some animals, create a bloody path with the parts of the animals, then each walk that path while making promises and calling a curse upon themselves if they failed to keep those promises. They might say, "Let me be cut asunder like these animals if I should fail to keep my promise to you."

We see a reference to this custom in Jeremiah 34:18–19. Here the Lord alludes to the fact that the leaders of Judah had passed between the pieces of a calf, and that He would do to them as was done to the calf since they did not keep their promise. The ESV is a little clearer in its translation of this verse. It reads:

"And the men who transgressed my covenant and did not keep the terms of the covenant that they made before me, I will make them like the calf that they cut in two and passed between its parts—the officials of Judah, the officials of Jerusalem, the eunuchs, the priests, and all the people of the land who passed between the parts of the calf" (Jer 34:18-19, ESV)

Ancient Near Eastern contracts were not sealed on paper. They were indelibly seared into the memories of the contracting parties. It would have been clear to Abram when God instructed him to cut the animals that God was going to cut a covenant with him. In the Hebrew language covenants are not said to be "signed" or "made." Rather, they are "cut." In verse 18, where we are told: "The LORD made a covenant with Abram", the word translated 'made' is the Hebrew כָּרַת (karath) which literally means 'cut'.

Abram did as God instructed. When birds such as vultures began to come down to feast on the carcases (v. 11), Abram did what he could to shoo them away. The props for signing the contract were set in place. But who were the parties of the covenant who would sign the contract?

Parties in the Covenant

We would expect that if God were cutting a covenant with Abram that God would be one party, and Abram would be the other. But verse 12 says: "And when the sun was going down, a deep sleep fell upon Abram; and, lo, an horror of great darkness fell upon him."

Abram fell into a deep sleep! Or perhaps he fell into a trance and found himself unable to move though He seemed to be aware of what was going on.

Moses in recording the event would have us know with certainty that Abram did not pass through the pieces. He was in a deep sleep! He was enveloped by an horror of great darkness.

Who then passed through the pieces? Verse 17 says: "And it came to pass, that, when the sun went down, and it was dark, behold a smoking furnace, and a burning lamp that passed between those pieces."

What passed through the pieces? A smoking furnace and a burning lamp! What are these? They are obviously symbolic and they have promoted many different interpretations. Most commentators believe that the two symbols represent two attributes or works of God. One commentator suggests that "the smoking furnace might be designed as an emblem of the sore afflictions of the Israelites in Egypt;

but the burning lamp was certainly the symbol of the Divine presence" (Clarke). Another commentator suggests, "The oven of smoke and lamp of flame symbolize the smoke of destruction and the light of salvation" (Barnes). Another says the smoking furnace symbolizes affliction in Egypt whereas the burning lamp shows comfort in affliction (Matthew Henry).

The problem with these interpretations, however, is that they overlook the significance of having the symbols pass through the pieces! Indeed, when they are interpreted the way that they are commonly interpreted, the key idea behind the whole vision would be lost and misunderstood!

You see, in the rite of covenant-cutting, it is the two parties making the covenant who pass through the pieces. When Abram saw the smoking furnace and burning lamp pass through the pieces, he would know that they represented the parties making the covenant! He would not think that they represented the content of the covenant or the circumstances surrounding it. Indeed, I am convinced that he also understood that they represented God. God passed through the pieces in two theophanies. A theophany is a symbolic appearance of God.

But why are there two distinct theophanies rather than one? When we compare Scripture with Scripture and are willing to let theology guide our understanding, the answer becomes obvious. In all likelihood, the smoking furnace represents God the Father, whereas the burning lamp represents God the Son. The Father provides us with daily bread. The Father's wrath will burn against sinners for all eternity. The Lord Jesus calls hell "a furnace of fire" in Matthew 13:42. Hell is hell not because the devil is there but because it is where the holy wrath of the Father against sin is constantly felt. The Lord Jesus, who is "the true Light, which lighteth every man that cometh into the world" (Jn 1:9) is no doubt represented by the burning lamp.

Who passed through the pieces? Who made the promises upon pain of death and destruction? It was not Abram, for he was in a deep sleep. It was, rather, God the Father and God the Son! What was enacted before Abram that day was no less than the everlasting Covenant of Grace between the Father representing the Triune Godhead and the Son representing His Church. The *Westminster Larger Catechism*, question 31, asks "With whom was the Covenant of Grace made?" The answer is: "The Covenant of Grace was made with Christ as the second Adam, and in him with all the elect as his seed."

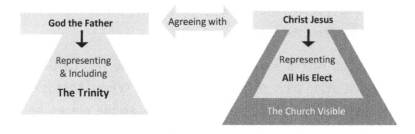

Figure 8: Parties of the Covenant of Grace

This enactment of cutting a covenant would convince Abram that God would keep His promise. But it has a far deeper significance. The apostle to the Hebrews speaks of it in chapter 6:

"For when God made promise to Abraham, because he could swear by no greater, he sware by himself, Saying, Surely blessing I will bless thee, and multiplying I will multiply thee. And so, after he had patiently endured, he obtained the promise. For men verily swear by the greater: and an oath for confirmation is to them an end of all strife. Wherein God, willing more abundantly to shew unto the heirs of promise the immutability of his counsel, confirmed it by an oath: That by two immutable things, in which it was impossible for God to lie, we might have a strong consolation, who have fled for refuge to lay hold upon the hope set before us" (Heb 6:13–18).

The two immutable things could refer to God's counsel and God's oath. But if the apostle has in mind the event of Genesis 15, it becomes very possible that he is referring to the two theophanies—the smoking furnace representing the Father and the burning lamp representing the Son.

When two parties pass through the pieces in the ancient covenant cutting rites, they are essentially saying: "Let me be cut asunder if I fail to keep my word." God is making this assertion. But as it is impossible that God would be destroyed, it is also impossible that God should fail to keep His promise.

As the Lord Jesus passed through the bloody pieces in the theophany, He was promising to pay for our violation of the covenant. In effect, He was saying, "Let me be cut asunder if I or my people break the covenant bond." The Lord Jesus had to die to fulfil the Covenant of Grace. You see, the Covenant of Grace is actually built upon the Covenant of Works. In the Covenant of Works, man is promised life upon perfect obedience to God's law. The Covenant of Works was never abrogated. So to have life, we must not only pay the penalty of breaking the Covenant of Works, but also fulfil its terms.

Fallen man cannot do so. But Christ is the perfect man. He was born of a virgin and so was not imputed with the guilt of Adam. Christ came to pay for our violation of the first covenant and to fulfil its terms. This is why He had to die. He was cut with the sword of the covenant for our sake. He died on the cruel cross and faced the immense wrath of the Father for our sin. After suffering the pains of hell on the cross, He gave up the ghost and died. But because His atonement was sufficient for us, He rose from the dead. Because He paid our debt for sin, His righteousness in keeping the law for us was accepted for procuring the promise of life for us. Christ Jesus kept the Covenant of Life on our behalf, and gave us the assurance that God's promises of salvation to us will never fail.

Promises of the Covenant

Let us now look at what God promised Abram. He says in verse 13:

"Know of a surety that thy seed shall be a stranger in a land that is not theirs, and shall serve them; and they shall afflict them four hundred years; And also that nation, whom they shall serve, will I judge: and afterward shall they come out with great substance. And thou shalt go to thy fathers in peace; thou shalt be buried in a good old age. But in the fourth generation they shall come hither again: for the iniquity of the Amorites is not yet full."

The covenantal promises are also stated in verse 18:

"In the same day the LORD made a covenant with Abram, saying, Unto thy seed have I given this land, from the river of Egypt unto the great river, the river Euphrates: The Kenites, and the Kenizzites, and the Kadmonites, And the Hittites, and the Perizzites, and the Rephaims. And the Amorites, and the Canaanites, and the Girgashites, and the Jebusites."

As usual, the promise made to Abram was couched in typical language. The promises would be fulfilled literally and they would also be fulfilled spiritually. Literally, God was telling Abram that his descendants would one day go into captivity for four hundred years; then come out of slavery with great wealth and inherit the land which God had promised Abram. This promise was fulfilled when Abram's children went into Egypt and remained there for four hundred years until God brought them out of captivity under the leadership of Moses. Eventually under the rule of King Solomon, Abram's children would have dominion over the territory from the river of Egypt unto the Euphrates (v. 18); or from Tipsah to Azza as stated in 1 Kings 4:21–24. God's promise to Abram has already been fulfilled literally. Those who say that it would be fulfilled in future when the nation of

Israel will again have her borders enlarged to stretch between the Nile to the Euphrates have, in my opinion, misunderstood scripture.

But let us understand that though the promise was fulfilled literally, it has also spiritual significance, for Egypt represents the darkness of sin and the world. So in this promise God was telling Abram that his seed would be redeemed out of sin and given an eternal inheritance in Christ. This was affirmed by Zacharias, the father of John the Baptist as he anticipated the birth of the Messiah. We read in Luke 1:67–75:

> *"And [John's] father Zacharias was filled with the Holy Ghost, and prophesied, saying, Blessed be the Lord God of Israel; for he hath visited and redeemed his people, And hath raised up an horn of salvation for us in the house of his servant David; As he spake by the mouth of his holy prophets, which have been since the world began: That we should be saved from our enemies, and from the hand of all that hate us; To perform the mercy promised to our fathers, and to remember his holy covenant; The oath which he sware to our father Abraham, That he would grant unto us, that we being delivered out of the hand of our enemies might serve him without fear, In holiness and righteousness before him, all the days of our life."*

Zacharias is clearly referring to Genesis 15 in which God swore to Abraham that Israel would be redeemed out of Egypt after four hundred years (Gen 15:13–14). But he also declares that the prophecy would be fulfilled in the coming of Messiah to redeem His people from sin (Lk 1:67). What this shows us, surely, is that the redemption of Israel out of Egypt as recorded in the book of Exodus is *not* the ultimate fulfilment of God's covenantal promise to Abraham. The ultimate fulfilment is found in the redemption of the Israel of God out of Spiritual Egypt by the Messiah. The exodus was but a type; while the spiritual redemption of God's people is the anti-type. The exodus fulfilled the promise in Genesis 15 typically, while redemption in Christ fulfils it ultimately.

Conclusion

The Covenant of Grace is not an invention of theologians. It is not merely a theory. It is a reality in the mind of God. It is a relational framework which God appointed to comprehend our salvation in Christ. But it is more than that. It is also an unbreakable bond of love between the Father and Son by which the people represented by the Son may enjoy eternal fellowship with God.

This covenant redounds to the glory of God. It fulfils His justice while demonstrating His mercy, grace and love towards us. It is the basis of the benediction that every beloved child of God may receive with confidence:

> *"Now the God of peace, that brought again from the dead our Lord Jesus, that great shepherd of the sheep, through the blood of the everlasting covenant, Make you perfect in every good work to do his will, working in you that which is wellpleasing in his sight, through Jesus Christ; to whom be glory for ever and ever. Amen"* (Heb 13:20–21).

7. THE COVENANT OF GRACE

We have shown how the covenant cut in Genesis 15 is best understood as a symbolic dramatisation of the Covenant of Grace. We will leave a detailed study of this Covenant for the next chapter where we will consider what the *Westminster Confession of Faith* teaches about it. But for now, we want to summarise briefly what the Covenant of Grace is.

Let us begin by reiterating that the Covenant of Grace was made in eternity past, even before the Covenant of Works was made with Adam, but it is logically founded upon Covenant of Works and is administered in redemptive history after the Fall. It is therefore loosely known as a second covenant (*WSC* 20). The first covenant was made with Adam, the second covenant was made with Christ as the second or last Adam (1 Cor 15:22, 45).

We say that this second covenant is founded upon the first because it requires Christ, on behalf of His elect, to fulfil the condition of the first, —namely perfect obedience of God's Law, —to procure life for them under its stipulations; as well as to pay the debt they owe under the same covenant. This would be so because the elect, though chosen in eternity, would existentially be represented first by Adam in the Fall and are therefore covenant debtors when Christ fulfilled the covenant on their behalf, as their Redeemer. Thus:

	Covenant of Works	**Covenant of Grace**
Parties	God & Mankind represented by Adam	God & the Elect represented by Christ
Condition	Perfect Obedience	(1) Pay for Penalty due to Covenant of Works violation; (2) Keep Covenant of Works
Blessing	Eternal Life	Per Covenant of Works
Curse	Eternal Death	Per Covenant of Works

Under the administration of this covenant in the life of the elect, God requires the elect to exercise faith that they may be united to Christ, their covenant head and so receive the benefits which He has procured for them. But in so far as this faith is a gift of God (Eph 2:8), we may conclude that it is part of the condition that God has imposed upon himself under the Covenant of Grace. Or if you like, we may say that it is part of God's unconditional promise to the elect. Why do we not say that it is part of God's promise of the covenant? Because the promise in the covenant is really the blessing that comes about through keeping the condition of the covenant! Remember that the condition of the Covenant of Grace is fulfilled in Christ. Thus, the Covenant of Grace may be represented thus (Figure 9):

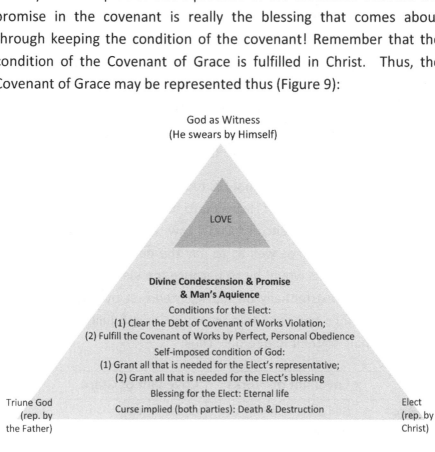

God as Witness
(He swears by Himself)

LOVE

**Divine Condescension & Promise
& Man's Aquience**
Conditions for the Elect:
(1) Clear the Debt of Covenant of Works Violation;
(2) Fulfill the Covenant of Works by Perfect, Personal Obedience

Self-imposed condition of God:
(1) Grant all that is needed for the Elect's representative;
(2) Grant all that is needed for the Elect's blessing

Blessing for the Elect: Eternal life
Curse implied (both parties): Death & Destruction

Triune God
(rep. by
the Father)

Elect
(rep. by
Christ)

Figure 9: *Covenant of Grace:*
A bond of love sealed by promissory oaths
(With conditions wholly fulfilled by Christ)

8. CONFESSIONAL TESTIMONY

Having briefly summarised what we may deduce from the Scripture on the Covenant of Grace, let us now consider how the *Westminster Confession of Faith* deals with the subject by drawing together various Scripture texts that reveal aspects of the same truth.

First consider the *WCF* 7.3, which states:

> *Man, by his fall, having made himself incapable of life by that covenant, the Lord was pleased to make a second, commonly called the Covenant of Grace: wherein He freely offereth unto sinners life and salvation by Jesus Christ, requiring of them faith in Him, that they may be saved; and promising to give unto all those that are ordained unto eternal life His Holy Spirit, to make them willing and able to believe.*
>
> *Gal 3:21; Rom 8:3; 3:20–21; Gen 3:15; Isa 42:6; Mk 16:15–16; Jn 3:16; Rom 10:6, 9; Gal 3:11; Ezk 36:26–27; Jn 6:44–45.*

Many, if not the majority[8] of, Reformed theologians today speak of a pre-temporal intra-Trinitarian Covenant of Redemption in which the persons of the Godhead covenanted with one another to bring an elect people unto adoption and the full enjoyment of God for all eternity. The Covenant of Redemption would, in this scheme, come to historical fruition through the Covenant of Works and the Covenant of Grace.

---

[8] Indeed, this has become so much the majority report that many cannot conceive of another way of presenting covenant theology. No less than the eminent modern Theologian, Dr J.I. Packer has remarked that "The full reality of God and God's work are not adequately grasped till the Covenant of Redemption –the specific covenantal agreement between Father and Son on which the Covenant of Grace rests –occupies its proper place in our minds" (Packer in Introduction to Herman Witsius, *Economy of the Covenants Between God and Man: Comprehending a Complete Body of Divinity* [Escondido, California: The den dulk Christian Foundation, Reprinted 1990], xv.).

In such a scheme, the Covenant of Grace is generally seen as being made with sinners in time, and conditioned upon faith. In other words, only those who exercise faith may enter into a covenant relation with God. This faith is provided to the elect as a gift that comes with the fulfilment of Covenant of Redemption by Christ.

Remarkably, however, although the framers of the Westminster Standards (1647) were aware of this three-covenant view, they chose to present the doctrine of redemption under a two-covenant framework without even referring explicitly to the "Covenant of Redemption."[9] No doubt, what is known as the Covenant of Redemption is, in their reckoning, really the essence of the Covenant of Grace, and cannot be fully distinguished from it. This one covenant combines the covenant between the Persons of the Godhead and God's covenant with the elect. In this framework, the Covenant of Grace is a covenant between God and His elect, with Christ, the God-Man, as their Representative.

The *Westminster Larger Catechism*, Q. 31 makes this clear. In answer to the question "With whom was the Covenant of Grace made?" the catechism says: "The Covenant of Grace was made with Christ as the second Adam, and in Him with all the elect as His seed." The Covenant of Works was made with Adam as a representative of all mankind, so it was made with him and all his posterity. In the same way, the Covenant of Grace is made with Christ, the second Adam, as the representative of His elect, so it was made with Him and His seed (see Gal 3:16; Rom 5:15ff.; Isa 53:10–11). It is, as such, an unconditional covenant as far as the elect are concerned, although it is, in a sense, conditioned upon Christ's fulfilment of the Covenant of Works as well as payment of the debt of sin on behalf of the elect.

---

9 See Andrew A Woolsey, *A Study in the Reformed Tradition to the Westminster Assembly* [RHB, 2012], 58-9.

This is elaborated in *WCF* 7:3, which may be comprehended and enlarged in the following 8 propositions:

1. This covenant was made between God the Father, representing the entire Godhead, and His co-eternal Son, who was to assume, in the fullness of time, a human nature in His Person, and to represent all His elect as their Mediator and Surety. This is taught in various passages in Scripture:

   • Psalm 89:3, 4: "I have made a covenant with my chosen, I have sworn unto David my servant, Thy seed will I establish for ever, and build up thy throne to all generations."

   This psalm, like other psalms, refers to David as a type of Christ, the Greater David or the Root of David (Rev 5:5). Scripture clearly intimates that the covenant was made with Christ rather than merely with David, for long after David was dead and buried, Ezekiel prophesied, "And I will set up one shepherd over them, and he shall feed them, even my servant David; he shall feed them, and he shall be their shepherd. ... And David my servant shall be king over them; and they all shall have one shepherd: they shall also walk in my judgments, and observe my statutes, and do them" (Ezk 34:23, 37:24; cf. Jer 30:9; Lk 24:44).

WCF 7.3 & Implications on the Covenant of Grace
• *Made between the Father and Son*
• *The Son represents the elect*
• *Established in eternity*
• *Entirely gratuitious*
• *Conditional for Christ, but unconditional for the elect*
• *Self-imposed condition on God's part includes all that is needed by the elect and their Representative.*
• *Faith by which the elect enjoys Christ's procured benefits is part of this grant.*

   • Isaiah 42:6–7: "I the LORD have called thee in righteousness, and will hold thine hand, and will keep thee, and give thee for a covenant of the people, for a light of the Gentiles; To open the blind eyes, to bring out the prisoners from the prison, and them that sit in darkness out of the prison house."

This verse clearly refers to Christ (cf. Isa 42:1–3 with Mt 12:18–21). It teaches us that the Covenant is a covenant of redemption of sinners from sin and Satan.

2. This covenant was made with Christ as the Head, or representative, of His spiritual seed. This is clearly taught by the apostle Paul in his comparisons between Adam and Christ:

"Wherefore, as by one man sin entered into the world, and death by sin; and so death passed upon all men, for that all have sinned: ...But not as the offense, so also is the free gift. For if through the offense of one many be dead, much more the grace of God, and the gift by grace, which is by one man, Jesus Christ, hath abounded unto many. ... Therefore as by the offense of one judgment came upon all men to condemnation; even so by the righteousness of one the free gift came upon all men unto justification of life" (Rom 5:12, 15, 18).

Just as Adam represented his posterity in death, Christ represents His elect in life. Christ indeed may be called the Second Adam. As 1 Corinthians 15:45 and 47 put it: "The first man Adam was made a living soul; the last Adam was made a quickening spirit. ... The first man is of the earth, earthy: the second man is the Lord from heaven."

Furthermore, the identity of Christ and His Church through covenant union is clearly taught in the Scripture. They are even identified by the same name: "And said unto me, Thou art my servant, O Israel, in whom I will be glorified" (Isa 49:3). When Saul persecuted the church, the Lord asked him: "Saul, Saul, why persecutest thou me?" (Acts 9:4)

Christ is also called the Surety of the Covenant, for Hebrews 7:22 says, "By so much was Jesus made a surety of a better testament." A surety is a person who takes upon himself the legal obligations of another. The promises of the covenant were primarily made with Christ as Surety: "Now to Abraham and his seed were the promises made. He saith not, And to seeds, as of many; but as of one, And to thy seed, which is Christ" (Gal 3:16). These promises were not made when the covenant was enacted in Genesis 15; they were made before the foundation of the world. Notice the allusion to the Covenant when Paul speaks of the "hope of eternal life, which God, that cannot lie, promised before the world began" (Tit 1:2).

3. This covenant was established from eternity. The Covenant of Grace is called a "second" covenant in our Confession because it is second in respect to *manifestation* and *execution* when compared with the Covenant of Works. Yet, in respect to *logical* and *temporal* order of conception and establishment, it is the first covenant. Christ, the embodiment of Wisdom, says, "I was set up from everlasting, from the beginning, or ever the earth was" (Prov 8:23). Robert Shaw is surely right to observe that Christ is saying that "he was set apart to his mediatory office and work, in other words, to be the head of his spiritual seed in the Covenant of Grace from everlasting."[10] Thus Christ in His earthly ministry made constant reference to a previous commission He had received of His Father (Jn 10:18, 17:4–5; Lk 22:29). And Paul tells us that eternal life was "promised before the world began" (Tit 1:2). Thus the Covenant of Grace is called an "everlasting covenant" (Heb 13:20).

---

[10] Robert Shaw, *An Exposition of the Westminster Confession of Faith* (Ross-shire: Christian Focus Publications, 1992 [1845]), 90–91; cf. Ps 2:6–8.

4. This covenant originated in the good pleasure of God's sovereign will and is completely gratuitous. As Paul says in Ephesians 1:3–6:

   "Blessed be the God and Father of our Lord Jesus Christ, who hath blessed us with all spiritual blessings in heavenly places in Christ: According as he hath chosen us in him before the foundation of the world, that we should be holy and without blame before him in love: Having predestinated us unto the adoption of children by Jesus Christ to himself, according to the good pleasure of his will, To the praise of the glory of his grace, wherein he hath made us accepted in the beloved."

5. While the Covenant of Grace seen from the standpoint of it being a relationship between God and the elect is unilateral (since its conditions will be kept by God) and unconditional (to man), when seen as an agreement between God and the Son, it is neither unilateral nor unconditional. The conditions or requirements of this Covenant are:

   a. That Christ should fulfil the Covenant of Works on behalf of His elect. In this sense, the Covenant of Grace is the continuation of the Covenant of Works. God the Son would assume human nature with its infirmities, yet be without sin. He would be born of a virgin. This is asserted in Galatians 4:4–5, Hebrews 2:10 and 4:15. He would place Himself under the law to keep it perfectly and so merit salvation on behalf of His elect. The Lord himself says in Matthew 5:17–18:

      "Think not that I am come to destroy the law, or the prophets: I am not come to destroy, but to fulfil. For verily I say unto you, Till heaven and earth pass, one jot or one tittle shall in no wise pass from the law, till all be fulfilled" (cf. Ps 40:8; Jn 8:29).

   b. That Christ should bear the iniquities of His elect by dying a propitiatory death for them, thus receiving the curse due to them for violating the Covenant of Works. This is clearly taught in Isaiah 53:10–11:

"Yet it pleased the LORD to bruise him; he hath put him to grief: when thou shalt make his soul an offering for sin, he shall see his seed, he shall prolong his days, and the pleasure of the LORD shall prosper in his hand. He shall see of the travail of his soul, and shall be satisfied: by his knowledge shall my righteous servant justify many; for he shall bear their iniquities."

Verse 10 has been beautifully paraphrased to read: "If His soul shall make a propitiatory sacrifice, he shall see a seed which shall prolong their days; and the gracious purpose of Jehovah shall prosper in His hands" (cited by Shaw, 90). See also John 10:17–18.

c. That Christ should apply His merits to His elect by regenerating them, endowing them with faith, and sanctifying them through the work of the Holy Spirit, thus securing the consecration of their lives to God. That this is the work of Christ is clearly seen in John 17:19–22:

"And for their sakes I sanctify myself, that they also might be sanctified through the truth. Neither pray I for these alone, but for them also which shall believe on me through their word; That they all may be one; as thou, Father, art in me, and I in thee, that they also may be one in us: that the world may believe that thou hast sent me. And the glory which thou gavest me I have given them; that they may be one, even as we are one."

That this is worked through the Holy Spirit may be seen in John 16:13–15.

6. The grant, self-imposed condition or the unconditional promise of the Covenant, which the Father makes on behalf of the entire Godhead, include the following:

   a. He would prepare for Christ a body uncontaminated by sin (Heb 10:5) and would anoint Him by giving Him the Spirit without measure, thus qualifying Him for the Messianic office (Isa 42:1–2; 61:1; Jn 3:34).

   b. He would support Christ in His work (Isa 42:6–7; Lk 22:43).

   c. He would deliver Christ from the power of death and highly exalt Him over all power in heaven and earth (Ps 16:8–11; Acts 2:25–28; Phil 2:9–11).

   d. He would enable Christ, on the basis of His fulfilling the conditions of the covenant, to send out the Holy Spirit for the formation of His spiritual body by the regeneration and sanctification of His elect, and for the instruction, guidance, and protection of His church so constituted (Jn 6:37, 39–40, 44–45; 14:26; 15:26; 16:13–14). This is the aspect emphasised in our Confession, which notes that God promises "to give unto all those that are ordained unto life His Holy Spirit, to make them willing and able to believe."

7. In the administration of this Covenant, *God* "freely offereth unto sinners life and salvation by Jesus Christ, requiring of them faith in Him, that they may be saved." It must be carefully noted that the faith in Christ that is referred here is, strictly speaking, not a condition, stipulation or requirement of the Covenant—if we understand such a condition, stipulation or requirement as *meritorious*. Rather, faith is presented here as the instrument or means of obtaining the salvation already procured by Christ. The condition of the Covenant, —as far as it pertains to the human

party, —is wholly fulfilled by Christ. It is true that *WLC* 32 speaks of "requiring faith as the condition to interest them in Him." But this must be read carefully in context, for it is a participial clause to the phrase that God "promiseth and giveth His Holy Spirit to all His elect, to work in them that faith, with all other saving graces...." In other words, the emphasis of this statement is the work of the Spirit. The present section in the Confession echoes that in saying that God promises "to give unto all those that are ordained unto eternal life His Holy Spirit, to make them willing, and able to believe." In other words, we may say that the provision of faith is part of God's unconditional promise, or if you like, God's self-imposed condition of the covenant!

It is Arminianism that teaches that faith is a condition of the Covenant of Grace which is imposed upon man. But if that is true, then the Covenant of Grace is no longer gracious, for though the provisions of the covenant may make it easier for the sinner to repent and believe in Christ (as the Arminians claim), it is ultimately still a work of obedience on the part of the sinner. As Paul puts it:

"If by grace, then is it no more of works: otherwise grace is no more grace. But if it be of works, then is it no more grace: otherwise work is no more work" (Rom 11:6)

Note, however, that there is a sense, from a human perspective, in which both faith and obedience are required of Christ's elect. This requirement is not meritorious but instrumental and preceptive. In regard to faith, the elect will live as strangers of the covenant until by faith they accept the covenant and its promises; at which time, they enter into the life of the covenant as its members. In regard to obedience, all members of the covenant must, according to the principle of new life within them, consecrate themselves to God in new obedience to walk by faith and gratitude as God's covenant people. Thus being in the Covenant of Grace does not imply being without personal responsibility. But from the divine perspective, the faith and obedience of covenant people belongs to the promissory part of the Covenant rather than its stipulations.

8. The penalty of failure to fulfil the requirements of the Covenant is implied in Hebrews 6:17–18 which says,

"Wherein God, willing more abundantly to shew unto the heirs of promise the immutability of his counsel, confirmed it by an oath: That by two immutable things, in which it was impossible for God to lie, we might have a strong consolation, who have fled for refuge to lay hold upon the hope set before us."

This passage, as we have already seen, refers to Genesis 15, when God cut a covenant with Abraham—which is really a symbolic dramatisation or re-affirmation of the Covenant of Grace already in force. In that display, God alone passed through the pieces of the animals, signifying that He would be destroyed if He fails to keep His covenant, which is, of course, impossible. The two immutable things which the author of Hebrews refer to are probably the Father represented by the smoking furnace (cf. Mt 13:42) and Christ represented by the burning lamp (Jn 1:9).

9. THE OLD COVENANT

We have considered how the Covenant of Grace is dramatised in Genesis 15, and how it is alluded to and used theologically in various other passages of Scripture. Now we must demonstrate how the Covenant of Grace undergirds all of God's dealings with His people throughout the ages.

The *Westminster Confession of Faith* offers a couple of succinct paragraphs on this subject. In the first place, *WCF* 7.5 states:

> *This covenant [i.e. the Covenant of Grace] was differently administered in the time of the law, and in the time of the gospel: under the law it was administered by promises, prophecies, sacrifices, circumcision, the paschal lamb, and other types and ordinances delivered to the people of the Jews, all fore-signifying Christ to come; which were, for that time, sufficient and efficacious, through the operation of the Spirit, to instruct and build up the elect in faith in the promised Messiah, by whom they had full remission of sins, and eternal salvation; and is called the Old Testament.*
>
> *2 Cor 3:6–9; Heb 8; 9; 10; Rom 4:11; Col 2:11–12; 1 Cor 5:7; 1 Cor 10:1–4; Heb 11:13; Jn 8:56; Gal 3:7–9, 14.*

There is only one Covenant of Grace which was administered differently in the Old and New Testaments. In Scripture such as Hebrews 8:13, the Old and New Testaments are known as the Old Covenant and the New Covenant. The Greek word for covenant is the same as that for testament (διαθήκη, *diathēkē*). The old and new covenants are called such to indicate their differences with respect to the Incarnation. But note that in all essential respects, they are the same:

(a) Christ is the Saviour of men before and after His advent, and He saves them the same way, by grace through faith in Him. So Christ is said to be "the Lamb slain from the foundation of the world"

(Rev 13:8). He is also the propitiation for sins committed under the old covenant (Rom 3:25; Heb 9:15). Thus, Christ was exhibited typically in all the ceremonial, but especially in the sacrificial system of the tabernacle and temple (Col 2:17; Heb 10:1–10). These Old Testament sacrifices and ceremonies were "sufficient and efficacious, through the operation of the Spirit" on the basis of their sacramental union with the incarnational work of Christ.

(b) Faith in Christ was the *instrumental* cause of salvation in the Old and New Testaments: "the just shall live by his faith" (Hab 2:4; cf. Ps 2:12; Rom 1:17; Gal 3:11; Heb 10:38). This is why the Old Covenant believers can be set forth as examples of faith (see Rom 4 and Heb 11). The same promises of spiritual grace and eternal blessedness were administered then and now (cf. Gen 17:7 with Mt 22:32; Gen 22:18 with Gal 3:16; see also Isa 43:25–27; Ezk 36:27; Job 19:25–27; Dan 12:2–3).

The Covenant of Grace was administered in the Old Testament in types and shadows that pointed to Christ and His work of atonement. The covenant is administered in the New Testament in ordinances founded upon the finished work at the Cross. We will see more of this in *WCF* 7.6 in the next chapter. But for now, it is instructive to note how the paragraph concludes with these words: "There are not therefore two covenants of grace differing in substance, but one and the same under various dispensations."

What are the various dispensations? Apart from the Old Testament and New Testament, one cannot fail to see that there are also various covenants between God and His people mentioned in the inspired records of the historical progress of the Church underage in the Old Testament.

What is the relationship between these covenants and the Covenant of Grace? A careful study of these covenants reveals that they are all historical administrations of the same Covenant of Grace! We may say that these historical covenants are really subordinate covenants of the Covenant of Grace. In other words, the Covenant of Grace is worked out or administered through subordinate covenants, each one continuing the same theme of redemption, but in increasing fullness and clarity. We may also think of the Covenant of Grace as a man walking through history, and each of the subordinate covenants as an outer jacket worn by the man. One by one, these jackets are shed until the New Covenant is revealed.

At the heart of each of these subordinate covenants is the Covenant of Grace. The subordinate covenants are to the Church Visible (comprising all who profess true religion and their children) as the Covenant of Grace is to the Church Invisible (comprising the elect). Or to put it in another way, while membership of the Covenant of Grace comprises all the elect, the membership of subordinate covenants comprises all who profess true religion and their children at the point in history. Thus, for example, children of believers today may or may not be members of the Covenant of Grace, but are all members of the New Covenant unless they are excluded by a refusal by their parents to have them receive the sign and seal of the covenant.

In any case, the promise of the Covenant of Grace when it is highlighted in a subordinate covenant (e.g. Abrahamic and New Covenant) is really only for the elect. Thus, when Peter says at his inaugural sermon: "the promise is unto you, and to your children" (Acts 2:39), we must understand that he is referring only to the elect children. Thus, we conclude that a believer will have elect descendants (even if it happens that his immediate children turn out reprobate). But because the promise is issued under the administration of the Covenant of Grace, the believer hearing the promise may apply the promise to every one of his children (since they are in the church visible), and therefore seek to bring them up as covenant children (or members of the covenant) in the fear of the Lord. But the covenant children must be admonished to believe in the Lord and warned that if they do not and despise the promise, they will perish. In that sense, the promise may appear to be conditional to covenant children as covenant children, though it is always unconditional to the elect.

But let us also take note that the covenant administrations are actually structured covenantally, which is why we call them subordinate covenants. We may see these covenants as being between God and His external covenant people.[11] This is why, for example, the books of Leviticus and Deuteronomy are structured as covenant documents with emphasis on covenant conditions (eg. Lev 1-25; Dt 4-26), blessings (eg. Lev 26:1-13; Dt 28:1-14) and curses (eg. Lev 26:14-46; Dt 28:15-68). Notice how these blessings and curses relate more to the people's life upon the earth rather than to their eternal estate. To the degree that God's people observe the conditions, to the degree that they will enjoy God's temporal blessings as a people, and as individuals. Conversely, to the degree that God's people fail to observe these conditions, to the degree they will experience God's temporal curses as a people.

---

[11] The covenant administrations are sometimes mediated by the administrative representatives of Christ such as patriarchs, priests, judges, kings or ministers. But these mediators, unlike the representatives of the Covenant of Works and Covenant of Grace do not possess the quality of vicarious heads in that their obedience or disobedience to the covenant conditions, is not imputed to the people they represent; though their decisions sometimes impact the lives of the people whether individually or corporately. Thus the covenant administration is not said to be between God and the representatives of the people, but between God and the people.

10. COVENANTAL ADMINISTRATIONS

In the previous chapter, we learned how the Covenant of Grace is administered through several subordinate covenants as recorded in the historical accounts of God's dealings with His people in the Old Covenant. In this follow-up study, we will look at each of these subordinate covenants and see their significance as well as how they relate to one another.

There are five Old Testament subordinate covenants:

a. The Adamic Covenant, also known as the Covenant of Commencement. It is under this administration of the Covenant of Grace that the Messiah was first promised (see Gen 3:15).

b. The Noahic Covenant, also known as the Covenant of Preservation. This subordinate covenant announces the religious significance of blood for atonement (Cf. Gen 9:4; Lev 17:11) to clarify that salvation must be procured by the propitiatory death of the Messiah. It is also under this covenant that deliverance and preservation in Christ for God's people is promised.

c. The Abrahamic Covenant, also known as the Covenant of Promise. Under this administration, not only is the Covenant of Grace symbolically dramatised, but the sacrament of circumcision as a sign and seal of the covenant is introduced to mark out God's covenant people. It is also under this administration that land inheritance is set forth as a type of eternal spiritual inheritance (cf. Gen 12, 15).

d. The Mosaic Covenant, also known as the Covenant of Law. Under this covenant, the Ceremonial Law is set in place (Ex 24–30) to instruct God's people about the theology of the atonement, and to prepare them for the atoning work of the Messiah (Ex 24-30). At the same time, the Moral Law (Ex 19–20), which is a way of life for

God's people, is republished, summarized and codified so that God's people may be clear about their covenant responsibility of loving their Covenant God. In this way, clarity is also provided that God's people may know what is perfect obedience, and what is required of the Messiah when He comes to fulfil the Covenant of Works on behalf of His people.

e. The Davidic Covenant, also known as the Covenant of Kingdom, makes the kingship of Christ obvious (cf. 2 Sam 7:12–13).

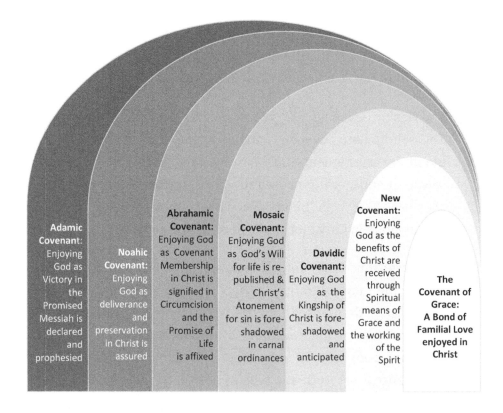

Figure 10: The Administrations of the Covenant of Grace

These are the five subordinate covenants under the Old Testament. But how do we know that they are indeed subordinate covenants related to each under the Covenant of Grace? How do we know that they are not unrelated and distinct dispensations, as some claim?

We know because their unity can be demonstrated from Scripture. In the first place, it is clear from Scripture that they share a *structural* unity; each covenant building on the previous ones. In the second place, these covenants have *thematic* unity for they all stress the same theme

a. With reference to *structural* unity, we see:

(a) The Lord referring to the Abrahamic Covenant at the inauguration of the Mosaic Covenant (see Ex 6:3–8);

(b) David, the inaugural member of the Davidic Covenant charging Solomon to keep the Mosaic Law (see 1 Kgs 2:3);

(c) Ezekiel mentioning most of the subordinate covenants in one breath, Ezekiel 37:24–26 says:

"And David my servant shall be king over them; and they all shall have one shepherd [alluding to Davidic Covenant]:...

they shall also walk in my judgments, and observe my statutes [Mosaic Covenant],...

and do them. And they shall dwell in the land that I have given unto Jacob my servant, wherein your fathers have dwelt; and they shall dwell therein, even they, and their children [Abrahamic Covenant],...

and their children's children for ever: and my servant David shall be their prince for ever. Moreover I will make a covenant of peace with them; it shall be an everlasting covenant with them: and I will place them, and multiply them, and will set my sanctuary in the midst of them for evermore."

b. As for *thematic* unity, we see the same theme, in each of the subordinate covenants. For example:

- In the Adamic Covenant, Genesis 3:15 states:

  "And I will put enmity between thee and the woman, and between thy seed and her seed; it shall bruise thy head, and thou shalt bruise his heel."

  The seed of the woman no doubt refers to Christ and the elect united to Him. The seed of the Serpent, on the other hand, refers to the Devil and all united to him. The seed of the Woman will have victory over the seed of the Serpent because God has declared it so. This verse implies God's ownership of His people even if that is not explicitly revealed.

- In the Abrahamic Covenant, we read in Genesis 17:7:

  "I will establish my covenant between me and thee and thy seed after thee in their generations for an everlasting covenant, <u>to be a God unto thee, and to thy seed after thee</u>. And I will give unto thee, and to thy seed after thee, the land wherein thou art a stranger, all the land of Canaan, for an everlasting possession; and <u>I will be their God</u>."

  Here, God's covenant ownership of His people is explicit and sealed with the sacrament of circumcision.

- In the Mosaic Covenant, we read in Exodus 6:6–7:

  "Wherefore say unto the children of Israel, I am the LORD, and I will bring you out from under the burdens of the Egyptians, and I will rid you out of their bondage, and I will redeem you with a stretched out arm, and with great judgments: And I will take you to me for a people, <u>and I will be to you a God: and ye shall know that I am the LORD your God</u>, which bringeth you out from under the burdens of the Egyptians."

Why does the Lord redeem Israel out of Egypt? Clearly it is to demonstrate His ownership of Israel as His people and to encourage the people to recognise Him as their God. Thus in Leviticus 26:12, God explicitly avows: "I will walk among you, and will be your God, and ye shall be my people."

In the Davidic Covenant, we see various allusions to the covenant theme. In particular, this theme is used whenever the covenant relationship between God and the people is restated and sealed by covenant-undertaking. For example, we read in 2 Kings 11:17:

"And Jehoiada made a covenant between the Lord and the king and the people, that they should be the Lord's people; between the king also and the people."

Conclusion

The numerous covenants in the Old Testament can be confusing for the average reader. But a deeper look at them while comparing Scripture with Scripture clearly reveals that all of these divine covenants flow out the eternal Covenant of Grace. More specifically, they are subordinate covenants designed to be temporal administrations of the eternal Covenant of Grace.

11. THE NEW COVENANT

We have seen how the divine covenants of the Old Testament are subordinates of the Covenant of Grace and are administered with different emphases to God's people living in different ages. We noted how these subordinate covenants are related to one another and to the Covenant of Grace by structure and theme. But what about the New Covenant prophesied in Jeremiah 31:33 and expounded in Hebrews 8 and 10?

It is not difficult to see how the New Covenant is also a subordinate covenant which is structurally and thematically united to the Old Testament subordinate covenants. Structurally, we see, for example, how the apostle Peter refers to the promise of the Abrahamic Covenant to instruct the inaugural new covenant congregation about repentance and baptism. He declares:

> "Repent, and be baptized every one of you in the name of Jesus Christ for the remission of sins, and ye shall receive the gift of the Holy Ghost. For the promise is unto you, and to your children, and to all that are afar off, even as many as the Lord our God shall call" (Acts 2:38–39).

It is not difficult to see that Peter is alluding to the Abrahamic Covenant (cf. Gen 17:7ff). We can see a promise implied in God' words to Abraham concerning the covenant:

> "And I will establish my covenant between me and thee and thy seed after thee in their generations for an everlasting covenant, to be a God unto thee, and to thy seed after thee" (Gen 17:7).

To establish the covenant in this context is not to make a fresh covenant, but to bless on the basis of the covenant. In other words, God promised to bless Abraham and his descendants (and all whom He would cause to be joined unto them, cf. Gen 12:3, 17:12b; 17:16).

Peter and his Jewish audience would have understood that this is *the* Promise of God. Indeed, every Jew who hears about an unqualified promise of God to him and his children, would automatically link it to the Abrahamic Covenant! This explains why Peter can speak about *the* Promise without explaining what promise he is referring to. Remarkably, Peter appears to be equating the promise of the Abrahamic Covenant with the promise of the Holy Spirit, thereby suggesting the promised blessing of the Abrahamic Covenant is really the Holy Spirit. Or to put it in another way, the promise of the Holy Spirit in the New Covenant is really the promise of the Abrahamic covenant, making them, in essence, the same.

It is instructive to note how the apostle Paul also refers to the Holy Spirit as being promised under the Abrahamic covenant. After speaking about Christ meeting the demand of the Mosaic Covenant, he says:

> *"Christ hath redeemed us from the curse of the law, being made a curse for us: for it is written, Cursed is every one that hangeth on a tree: That the blessing of Abraham might come on the Gentiles through Jesus Christ; that we might receive the promise of the Spirit through faith" (Gal 3:13-14).*

There is no question, therefore, that the New Covenant is structurally united and, in essence, the same as the Old Testament subordinate covenants.

As for thematic unity between the Old and New covenants, consider how Paul appeals to the theme of the Old Covenant as stated under the Mosaic Covenant (see Lev 26:12) to urge the New Testament saints to live holy lives, separate from the world:

> *"Be ye not unequally yoked together with unbelievers: for what fellowship hath righteousness with unrighteousness? and what communion hath light with darkness? And what concord hath Christ*

with Belial? or what part hath he that believeth with an infidel? And what agreement hath the temple of God with idols? for ye are the temple of the living God; as God hath said, I will dwell in them, and walk in them; and I will be their God, and they shall be my people" (2 Cor 6:14–16).

Clearly the New Covenant is not entirely new. It is better (Heb 7:22; 8:6) not in the sense of being entirely new, but in the sense that it reveals, in clarity, the substance of what is pointed in the Old Covenant in shadows and types. Thus, the *Westminster Confession of Faith* states in chapter 7, paragraph 6:

> *"Under the gospel, when Christ, the substance, was exhibited, the ordinances in which this covenant is dispensed are the preaching of the Word, and the administration of the sacraments of Baptism and the Lord's Supper: which, though fewer in number, and administered with more simplicity and less outward glory, yet, in them, it is held forth in more fullness, evidence, and spiritual efficacy, to all nations, both Jews and Gentiles; and is called the New Testament. There are not therefore two covenants of grace differing in substance, but one and the same under various dispensations*
>
> Col 2:17; Mt 28:19–20; 1 Cor 11:23–25; Heb 12:22–27; Jer 31:33–34; Mt 28:19; Eph 2:15–19; Lk 22:20; Gal 3:14, 16; Acts 15:11; Rom 3:21–23, 30; Ps 32:1; Rom 4:3, 6, 16–17, 23–24; Heb 13:8.

The Covenant of Grace is administered in the New Covenant (known here as the gospel) in greater simplicity, clearness and fullness since Christ, the Anti-type (of the Old Covenant types), has completed His work of redemption. The New Covenant is superior to the Old Covenant (encompassing all the subordinate covenants of the Old Testament) for the following reasons:

a. It is administered by Christ the Son, rather than servants such as Moses (cf. Heb 3:5–6).

b. Before, the truth was partly hidden, partly revealed in types and symbols, but now it is revealed in the clear history of the Incarnation together with the inspired commentary and explanation of the apostles.

c. The old administration was largely external, carnal, and ceremonial and involved land, temples, sacrifices, rituals, and feasts. But under the New Covenant, the administration becomes largely internal and spiritual, apart from the two sacraments, Baptism and the Lord's Supper.

d. The bloody signs and seals of the covenant under the Old Covenant administration, namely, Circumcision and the Passover have been replaced with the bloodless sacraments of Baptism and the Lord's Supper. Membership in the covenant had been largely confined to one people, but now it embraces people from all the earth without racial or geographic distinction.

e. The New Covenant involves internalisation of the Law through regeneration and indwelling of the Holy Spirit. The Lord said through Jeremiah "But this shall be the covenant that I will make with the house of Israel; After those days, saith the LORD, I will put my law in their inward parts, and write it in their hearts; and will be their God, and they shall be my people" (Jer 31:33; cf. Ezk 11:19).

    Under the Old Covenant, the Law of God was external and written on tablets of stones. In general, the members of the covenant, i.e. the Jews, had no power to keep the commandments. The ability to keep the law was not an intrinsic feature of the covenant. But with the New Covenant, the covenant members generally have the Law of God inscribed in their hearts. This is a graphic way of saying that the New Covenant includes regeneration and the indwelling of the Holy Spirit. Under the New Covenant, God's children will not only be regenerated, and thus be able to keep the Law, but also have the Holy Spirit indwelling them so they can discern spiritual matters.

Does that mean the Holy Spirit did not regenerate God's people in the Old Testament? John Calvin answers:

> "Was the grace of regeneration wanting to the Fathers under the Law? But this is quite preposterous. ...the Fathers, who were formerly regenerated obtained this favour through Christ, so that we may say, that it was as it were transferred to them from another source. The power then to penetrate into the heart was not inherent in the law, but it was a benefit transferred to the law from the Gospel."[12]

O. Palmer Robertson concurs:

> "Nothing under the Old Covenant had the effectiveness necessary actually to reconcile the sinner to God. Only in anticipation of the finished work of Christ could an act of heart-renewal be performed under the provisions of the Old Covenant"[13]

In other words, the saints of the Old Covenant were regenerated, but this benefit, strictly speaking, did not belong to the Old Covenant, for it was dependent on the finished work of Christ on the Cross. We can say that a regenerated Old Covenant saint is like a man who has completed all the requirements for a degree

---

[12] Calvin's *Comm. on Jer 31:33* (p. 131).

[13] O. Palmer Robertson, *The Christ of the Covenants* (Phillipsburg, New Jersey: Presbyterian and Reformed Publishing, 1980), 292.

programme even before the last course begins. For this reason, he begins to enjoy some of the benefits of a graduate, in view of the degree that will be conferred, even though the last course has not even started.

With this in mind, we may better understand what Jeremiah means when he adds in verse 34:

> "And they shall teach no more every man his neighbour, and every man his brother, saying, Know the LORD: for they shall all know me, from the least of them unto the greatest of them, saith the LORD."

Jeremiah is, no doubt, using hyperbole. We may say that it is both a qualitative and a quantitative hyperbole. Quantitatively, in God's appointment, there would be far fewer of God's elect, and therefore far fewer for whom this statement would be true amongst the visible membership of the Old Covenant compared to that of the New Covenant. Qualitatively, with the illuminating help of the Holy Spirit, New Covenant true believers would know much more and enjoy more fully the benefits purchased for them at the Cross than even the elect under the old economy. Figure 11 illustrates this difference graphically.

Covenant of Grace

Old Covenant		Benefits	New Covenant	
Sense	Availability		Availability	Sense
		Forgiveness of sin		
		Indwelling of Holy Spirit		
		Regeneration		
		Illumination		
		Sanctification		

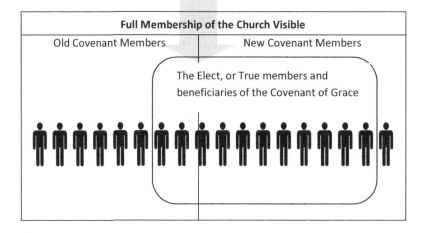

Full Membership of the Church Visible

Old Covenant Members   New Covenant Members

The Elect, or True members and beneficiaries of the Covenant of Grace

Key:

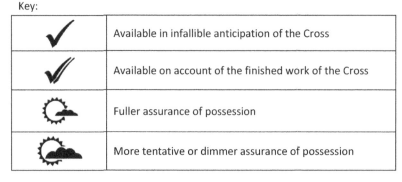

	Available in infallible anticipation of the Cross
	Available on account of the finished work of the Cross
	Fuller assurance of possession
	More tentative or dimmer assurance of possession

Figure 11: Difference between Old and New Covenant per Jeremiah 31:33-34

Conclusion

The *Westminster Shorter Catechism* refers to the New Covenant in a question regarding sacraments:

Q. 92. What is a sacrament?

A. A sacrament is an holy ordinance instituted by Christ; wherein, by sensible signs, Christ, and the benefits of the new covenant, are represented, sealed, and applied to believers.

Gen 17:7,10; Ex 12; 1 Cor 11:23, 26

We could say much about this statement, but what is relevant in the present context is that the sacraments of baptism and the Lord's Supper are holy ordinances by which the benefits of the New Covenant are represented, sealed, and applied to believers. These benefits, which include regeneration and sanctification, are not dispensed only in the New Covenant. They were also dispensed in the Old Covenant. So they are really benefits of the Covenant of Grace.

But if that is so, why does our catechism speak of them as benefits of the New Covenant? The answer is that the New Covenant is part of the Covenant of Grace. The Covenant of Grace is the essence of all subordinate covenants, including the New Covenant. The subordinate covenants are the temporal administration of the eternal Covenant of Grace. In the wisdom of God, the essence and benefits of the Covenant of Grace are not revealed all at once. They are rather revealed progressively through each succeeding covenant.

Think of the analogy of the man with many coats. The man is really Christ, because the substance of the Covenant of Grace is only found in Him. As this man walks through the redemptive history of God's people, he sheds his outer coat one at a time. Each time a coat is shed, some new information about the man is revealed. Each time a coat is shed, more light and more heat emanates from the man. But after the last coat is shed, Christ stands clothed in the New Covenant. Before that, we see Christ and His benefits through various layers of coat, but now we see Him and enjoy his benefits much more fully than before. Thus the benefits of the Covenant of Grace are rightly referred to as the benefits of the New Covenant.

12. IMPLICATIONS

We have learned how God deals with His people within the framework of the Covenant of Grace, which is administered through a series of subordinate covenants ending with the New Covenant. God's people today are still under the New Covenant. As we conclude, this series of studies let us consider the far-reaching implications of the doctrine.

Covenant Salvation

The first and perhaps most important implication of this doctrine is that there has been only one way of salvation since the Fall. Old Covenant saints and New Covenant alike are justified by grace through faith in the Lord Jesus Christ. Old Covenant saints were not saved by their works or by keeping the law. Likewise, New Covenant saints are not saved because of their faith. Faith is an instrument given by our Saviour and Covenant Representative to enable His elect throughout the ages to receive the benefits of salvation which He has procured for them by living and dying for them. He lived to keep the Covenant of Works on their behalf; He suffered and died to pay the penalty for their violation of the Covenant of Works.

Thus the apostle Paul reminds us that Christ "was delivered for our offenses, and was raised again for our justification" (Rom 4:25). He was not raised *in order* that we might be justified. He was raised because He has sufficiently paid for our sin. His resurrection secured our justification

The Covenant of Grace, we must remember, is gracious to us and therefore unconditional to us. It is not unconditional to Christ, for it was a Covenant of Works to Him, but it is

> **Implications of Covenant Theology**
> - Covenant Salvation
> - Covenant People
> - Covenant Ministry
> - Covenant Worship
> - Covenant Life
> - Covenant Sabbath
> - Covenant Membership
> - Covenant Family
> - Covenant Holiness
> - Covenant Responsibility
> - Covenant Love

unconditional for us. We do not contribute a stitch to the garment of our salvation. We do not lift a finger to assist or to promote our salvation. By God's grace, we are enabled by the power of the Spirit of Christ in our hearts to work out our salvation with fear and trembling (Phil 2:12–13). We do this out of gratitude and joy rather than obligation or duty.

Covenant People

The second implication of the Covenant of Grace is that God has only one covenant people. If there is only one Covenant of Grace and both the Old Covenant and the New Covenant are subordinate to it, it follows that the saints of the Old and New Covenant are one. God does not regard Israel as a distinct people and the church as another distinct people.

Those who are truly God's people are the elect. These may live under the Old Covenant or the New Covenant. Under the Old Covenant and prior to the Flood, the elect were mainly among the children of Seth, the son of Adam. At the time of the flood, they were only to be found in Noah's family. After the flood, the elect were found mostly in the line of Shem. Eventually, Abraham came onto the scene and the elect began to be found mostly in what would be known as the nation of Israel, in the line of Jacob, the son of Isaac, the son of Abraham. This would be so for almost two thousand years until the time of Christ. During this time, the nation of Israel was regarded as the covenant people of God for the elects' sake. Not everyone in Israel was truly the covenant people of God, for the covenant people of God are the elect. Israel would be nurtured by God's special providence like a garden in which his elect plants (Mt 15:13) would be cultivated. And so Israel was given all the laws and ordinances of God, as well as the gospel (Rom 9:4; Heb 4:2). Israel was, therefore, the external covenant people of God. She was the Church under age (*WCF* 19:3). She was beloved for the fathers' sake (Rom 11:28), because God had made a promise to Abraham, Isaac and Jacob particularly, that He would bless them, or more specifically, that His elect would be found amongst their descendants.

But Israel was increasingly unfaithful to the covenant. The people became more superstitious and idolatrous. They were religious and zealous, but in a superficial and superstitious way that eviscerated Christ from the ceremonies, ordinances, and Word that were delivered to them. Eventually, they rejected the Messiah, the covenant Head of God's people. They condemned Him to the cross and cried, "His blood be on us, and on our children" (Mt 27:25; cf. Acts 18:6). For this reason, the apostle Paul speaks of how the unbelieving branches were cut off from the olive tree (Rom 11:17-20). The olive tree represented the external covenant people of God.

As we enter into the New Covenant administration of the Covenant of Grace, the Olive Tree was lean and trim. The top-most branches comprised only the individuals and family that confessed that Jesus Christ was the Messiah. They were not necessarily all elect, for the apostle Paul reminds us that the branches of the Tree can still be cut off (Rom 11:22).

But from then on, the gospel went forth to people of other nations. It was preached first in Jerusalem, then in Judaea, then in Samaria, then to the uttermost parts of the world. Gentiles were gathered in in huge numbers. All who confessed Christ as Lord and Saviour were grafted to the Olive Tree and baptised. All their children were also baptised because they were part of the Olive Tree. Again, remember that they are not necessarily all elect, though the elect will be found amongst them. And we have reason to believe that because of the outpouring of the Holy Spirit at Pentecost, that the 'density' of the elect in the Olive Tree would be far greater than ever before under the Old Covenant.

Today, the covenant people of God are mostly Gentiles. These are the members of the true Church Universal and Visible (comprising all true churches). The Jews can still be grafted in again if they repent of their unbelief (Rom 11:23). But it is clear that that there is only one Olive Tree. God has only one external covenant people, just as Christ has only one body of the elect, the true covenant people of God. Israel today is not a holy nation; it is not part of the covenant people of God. For the sake of the fathers, there will no doubt be elect Jews who will be brought to faith. But when they are brought to faith, they will be brought in through the Church of Christ under the New Covenant administration of the Covenant of Grace.

Covenant Ministry

The third implication of covenant theology pertains to the ministry of the Word in the church. We noted that our covenant relationship with God is wholly purchased by Christ, guaranteed by the Father and effected by the Holy Spirit. Does that mean that the church should be entirely passive when it comes to the matter of salvation? Of course not! The apostle Paul reminds us that "whosoever shall call upon the name of the Lord shall be saved" (Rom 10:13), but how "shall they call on him in whom they have not believed? and how shall they believe in him of whom they have not heard?" (Rom 10:14). So there must be preachers and preaching. But who are preachers? and what should they preach?

Well, the answers are obvious and irrefutable as soon as we understand that Christ is the Covenant Head of the Church and that God has appointed His external covenant body (the Church Visible) to be the nursery in which the true members of covenant (the elect) are to be brought to a conscious union and communion with Him (review Figure 8). As soon as we understand this, we cannot but insist that the preacher is not only a herald of Christ to represent Him to call His sheep to himself, but also a preacher of Christ to teach the flock how to walk with Christ. Thus, the preacher must call and persuade all members of the covenant body to close with Christ. Of course, only the true members of the Covenant of Grace will be given faith by the Holy Spirit and therefore enabled truly to enjoy the blessings of the covenant in union and communion with Christ. But the preacher has only the sign and seal of the covenant to go by, and therefore must persuade every member of the body of the love of Christ for them, and of His kingly invitation to come unto Him. And yes, the sign and seal of the covenant, baptism, gives him the warrant to do so! He may be a bit more discretionary when it comes to addressing such as are unconverted and profess not Christ, but he must feel free to speak to the covenant community as the people of Christ even though some of them may well be reprobate.

Does that mean that the pastor of the church should only preach to the members of the church, or to the converted only? Of course not! In the first place, since salvation is generally offered under the administration of the covenant, it is imperative that churches go out of the way to make disciples of all men, that they may be saved. Thus, the Lord exhorts His disciples to go and make disciples[14] of all nations, baptising them in the name of the Father, the Son and the Holy Ghost and teaching them to observe all that He has commanded them (Mt 28:19-20). In the second place, as we saw previously, the covenant community (or local church assembly) includes those who are not yet converted. Therefore, it is imperative that all ministers preach experimentally and persuasively with a deep longing for the genuine conversion of all members of the church. In the third place, while it is true that the preaching ministry is not primarily a witness to the world, if the members of the church are faithful as witnesses in the world, as they should be, then there will always be the unlearned, unconverted

---

[14] Take note that the imperative translated "teach" in the KJV in Matthew 29:19 is the Greek μαθητεύω (mathēteuō), which literally means to "to disciple" or "to make disciple."

and strangers of the covenant (cf. 1 Cor 14:24) coming in to observe the worship of the Lord. Therefore, it is necessary a faithful preaching ministry be done with a heart for the conversion of all, whether in the world or in the church.

Of course, for this purpose, the minister must not only freely offer Christ and call for a closure with Him, he must also teach the flock their covenant responsibilities. It is only in walking according to their covenant responsibilities that they will work out their salvation with fear and trembling (Phil 2:13) and enter into a conscious enjoyment of the fellowship that their Covenant Head enjoys with the Father. "That which we have seen and heard declare we unto you, that ye also may have fellowship with us: and truly our fellowship *is* with the Father, and with his Son Jesus Christ" says the apostle John (1 Jn 1:3).

Covenant Worship

The fourth implication of the doctrine of the Covenant is that our worship must be covenantal. If our relationship to God is covenantal at heart, and is mediated by Christ our covenant Head, then surely our worship must be covenantal and mediated by Christ. The Lord Jesus says: "I am the way, the truth, and the life: no man cometh unto the Father, but by me" (Jn 14:6). This verse is often applied to our salvation, and rightly so. But it should be noted that our Lord is really referring to all manner of our relationship with God. Prayer is obvious. We must pray in the name of Christ. But what is often neglected is that all aspects of worship should also be through Him.

The modern church thinks of worship as a group of people doing what they think will please themselves and glorify God at the same time, while Christ stands by as a guest to grace the occasion. So a congregation transforms itself into a hundred– or a thousand – member choir to praise God, with Christ as a spectator. But this is wrong. The Lord himself teaches that He is not ashamed to call us brethren, saying, "I will declare thy name unto my brethren, in the midst of the church will I sing praise unto thee" (Heb 2:12). Christ is one of the worshipers! Indeed, we can only come unto the Father through His Son, who is the Head of the Church. He is the worshiper-in-chief. True worship is not accomplished by a great choir doing its best to please God. True worship happens when as the covenant people of God we stand behind Christ, our God-approved Soloist, as backup singers, singing His songs. This is why we sing the Psalms, "the word of Christ" (Col 3:16).

We read in Psalm 24:3–4: "Who shall ascend into the hill of the LORD? or who shall stand in His holy place? He that hath clean hands, and a pure heart; who hath not lifted up his soul unto vanity, nor sworn deceitfully." Who, we wonder, is such a man? For there is none righteous: no not one. Even our righteous works are filthy rags in God's sight. How can we then ascend unto God in worship? Thank God we can because Christ our Covenant Head qualifies, and He has redeemed us and gathered us, that we might stand behind Him to worship the Father through Him.

Covenant Life

The fifth implication of covenant theology is that church life should be covenantal. As the church worships as a covenant body, she should also live as a covenant body rather than merely as an occasional gathering. This is applicable in every local church, for the local church is a microcosm of the Church Universal, the body of Christ.

The Church Invisible Universal, which is comprised of the full number of the elect, is the true covenant body of Christ. The Church Visible Universal is the external covenant people of Christ in time, which serves as the wheat field in which the plantings of the Lord (i.e. the elect) are to be cultivated. The Church Universal Visible (comprising all the true branches of Christ) is therefore dealt with by God as the (external) covenant body of Christ. But it is practically impossible for the church throughout the world to function as one body. Therefore, it is clear that Paul's instruction in regard to the Church functioning as a body with many members (1 Cor 12:12-26) should be applied to every true Congregation of Christ. We will discuss this further in another chapter. But for now, it is helpful to consider how the local church should respond to God's Covenant of Grace by entering into what may be called church covenants.

Figure 12: *Church & Personal Covenants:*
where a desire to serve the LORD is sealed by promises or vows

When we talk about covenant or covenanting, in this sense, we are referring to vows made unto the Lord by God's people. We must not confuse such covenants with the Covenant of Grace in which Christ covenanted with the Father to redeem a people unto Himself. This Covenant of Grace is revealed in various subordinate covenants in Scripture, and is referred to by God as "my covenant" in numerous places (Gen 6:18; 9:11; 17:2, 4, 7, 10; Ex 6:4; 19:5; Jdg 2:1). This covenant is God's promise to redeem His people. The covenants we make with God, on the other hand, are promissory oaths (*WCF* 22.5), wherein as part of our religious worship, we solemnly call upon God to witness what we assert, or promise, and to judge us according to the truth and performance of what we have vowed (*WCF* 22.1).

Such covenants are evident throughout the history of God's people. During the reign of King Asa in Judah, for example, there was a great revival and reformation in which all the people "entered into a covenant to seek the LORD God of their fathers with all their heart and with all their soul" (2 Chr 15:12). Later, during the reign of King Josiah, the king read the rediscovered "book of the covenant" to the people and, acting as representative of his people, made a covenant before the LORD, "to walk after the LORD, and to keep His commandments and His testimonies and His statutes with all their heart and all their soul, to perform the words of this covenant that were written in this book" (2 Kgs 23:3). Note the distinction between the stipulation of God's covenant and the covenant that Josiah made on behalf of the people. This ecclesiastical covenanting was also evident during the time of Nehemiah, when the people, who were returning to Israel after exile, made a "sure covenant" that was written and sealed by the princes, Levites, and priests (Neh 9:38).

This is what we mean by Church covenants. As the Church, under age, under the administration of the Old Covenant made use of such covenant, so the Church under the administration of the New Covenant should make use of them that amongst other things, the members may be united together by covenant to make the covenant life of the church viable and enjoyable.

Covenant Sabbath

The sixth implication of the doctrine of the covenant is that God's people should keep the Sabbath as a covenant sign which identifies them as God's people. In Exodus 31:13-17, the Lord thus instructs Moses:

"Speak thou also unto the children of Israel, saying, Verily my sabbaths ye shall keep: for it is a sign between me and you throughout your generations; that ye may know that I am the LORD that doth sanctify you. Ye shall keep the sabbath therefore; for it is holy unto you: every one that defileth it shall surely be put to death:

for whosoever doeth any work therein, that soul shall be cut off from among his people. Six days may work be done; but in the seventh is the sabbath of rest, holy to the LORD: whosoever doeth any work in the sabbath day, he shall surely be put to death. Wherefore the children of Israel shall keep the sabbath, to observe the sabbath throughout their generations, for a perpetual covenant. ¹⁷ It is a sign between me and the children of Israel for ever: for in six days the LORD made heaven and earth, and on the seventh day he rested, and was refreshed."

Under the Old Covenant, the weekly Sabbath distinguished God's covenant people from other nations. It was an important ordinance to mark out the people who belonged to the LORD. What about under the New Covenant? Well, if the New Covenant and the Old Covenant are but different administration of the Covenant of Grace, then we should expect (by good and necessary consequences) that the covenant sign should remain, especially when it was instituted at creation rather than at the establishment of the nation of Israel (Gen 2:2-3). And this is exactly what we are told under the inspiration of the Holy Spirit, for we read in Hebrews 4:9, that "there remaineth therefore a rest to the people of God."

The word rendered "rest" here is the *hapax legomenon, σαββατισμός* (*sabbatismos*) which appears to have been created by the writer to speak of the weekly sabbath-rest in distinction from the general idea of rest. All the other occurrences of the word "rest" in the context are from the Greek word *κατάπαυσις* (*katapausis*).

It is clear, then, that the weekly Sabbath remains a covenant sign for God's people. God's people should keep the Sabbath as an emblem to identify themselves as the covenant people of God. They should keep it on the first day of the week, however, for it is on the first day of the week that Christ, their covenant head rose from the dead and was made the cornerstone of the church (Ps 118:22–24; cf. Acts 4:10–11).

Covenant Membership

The seventh implication of the doctrine of the covenant relates to baptism as a covenant sign of membership. God has appointed this visible sign and seal to mark His external covenant people. From the time of Abraham till the resurrection of Christ, the sign of the covenant was circumcision. Circumcision of the flesh pointed to circumcision of the heart, which is regeneration. Circumcision of the flesh signifies that a person belongs to the external covenant people of God (the Church Visible); just as circumcision of the heart signifies that a person belongs to the elect body of Christ (the Church Invisible).

Under the New Covenant, the bloody sacrament of circumcision was replaced by the bloodless sacrament of baptism. Water baptism points to baptism of the Spirit, which is also regeneration. Like circumcision of the flesh, baptism signifies that a person belongs to the external covenant people of God (the Church Visible). Like circumcision of the heart, baptism of the Spirit signifies that a person belongs to the elect body of Christ (the Church Invisible).

The apostle Paul alluded to the relationship between the two covenant signs when he reminded the Colossians that they were "circumcised with the circumcision made without hands," as they were "buried with [Christ] in baptism" (Col 2:11-12). The essential connection between the two sacraments is, therefore, clear. They have the same meaning. They have the same purpose. They are to be applied to the external covenant people of God, and they are, by the Spirit of Christ, efficacious only to those who are truly the covenant people of God, the elect.

That being the case, it is not difficult to see how baptism is to be applied as circumcision was. As infants of covenant members were circumcised under the Old Covenant, infants of covenant members under the New Covenant should be baptised. They were circumcised and now they are baptized to signify that they are members of the covenant by birth. Of course, under the Old Covenant only males were circumcised. But under the New Covenant, in which engrafting via conversion became a major mode by which the church grew, it became necessary that the sacrament be applied both to male and female. Thus Paul says:

> "For as many of you as have been baptized into Christ have put on Christ. There is neither Jew nor Greek, there is neither bond nor free, there is neither male nor female: for ye are all one in Christ Jesus. And if ye be Christ's, then are ye Abraham's seed, and heirs according to the promise" (Gal 3:27–29).

Baptism, like circumcision, does not guarantee salvation. But since it is a means of grace, ordinarily those who are *not* baptised have no assurance of salvation.

| | Membership Criterion | Ratification of Membership | | |
		Theological Terms	OT Terms	NT Terms
Church Invisible	Election	Regeneration	Heart Circumcision	Spirit Baptism
Church Visible	Profession of Faith, Covenant Birth	Sacrament for Ratification of Membership	Fleshly Circumcision	Water Baptism

Figure 13: The Relationship between Circumcision & Baptism

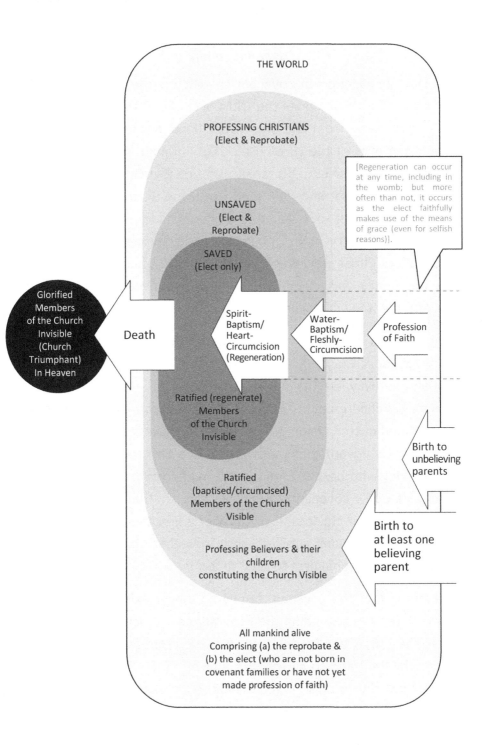

Figure 14: The *Ordinary* Progress of Grace

Covenant Family

The eighth implication of covenant theology is the covenant family. That concept is clear under the Old Covenant. For example, Noah's family was saved from the worldwide flood because "Noah found grace in the eyes of the Lord" (Gen 6:8). Abraham was instructed to circumcise all the males in his family as a sign that God would keep his covenant with him and his seed to come (Gen 17:10). Moses instructed the fathers of Israel to teach their children in the way of the Lord (Dt 6:1–10). For many generations, the primary mode in which the church of Christ grew was through the birth of covenant children. Thus the family was crucial in the outworking of God's covenant mercies under the Old Covenant.

Is the covenant family still important under the New Covenant? More specifically, does God still nurture His elect in Christian families? Or to put it another way, are the children of believers more likely to be elect compared to children of the world? Note that we are not talking about the likelihood of conversion, for children of believers would, of course, have a greater advantage by growing up in a Christian family. Rather, we are asking whether the family is still an important factor in the out-working of God's covenant so that we can say that the covenant is unto us and to our children. If the answer is yes, then it is meaningful to speak of "covenant families" and "covenant children." If not, it would be quite meaningless to use the terms.

Some argue that the covenant family no longer exists. They say the apostle Peter was extending the generational aspect of the covenant only to the Jews when he declared: "For the promise is unto you, and to your children, and to all that are afar off" (Acts 2:39a). Regarding the Gentiles, the promise extends only to "as many as the Lord our God shall call" (Acts 2:39b). Families are not included.

We believe this assertion is invalid for the following five reasons:

1. The concept of families and generations is intrinsic and cannot be extricated from God's plan for mankind. We see that in the way God has chosen to bring His elect into the world. He could have chosen to bring the elect into existence in an instant, as He did for the elect angels. We see this also in the annex to the second command in which God says:

> "*I the* LORD *thy God am a jealous God, visiting the iniquity of the fathers upon the children unto the third and fourth generation of them that hate me; And shewing mercy unto thousands of them that love me, and keep my commandments*" (Ex 20:5–6).

This will make no sense to believers who live in the New Covenant if God's promise no longer extends to their children.

2. God's continuing concern for the families of His people is indicated in the instances of household baptisms recorded in the New Testament. A case in point would be the baptism of the Philippian Jailer, a gentile together with his whole household.

3. The Old Testament practice of counting families and not just individuals carries into the New Testament. For example, when Luke recorded the number of people who were added to the church at Pentecost, he used the word *souls* (ψυχή, *psuchê*). In all probability, he used this word because he was counting men, women, and children. But two chapters later, Luke says that five thousand *men* were added to the church (Acts 4:4). That reminds us of Luke's reference to the Lord's feeding of five thousand men (Lk 9:14). Matthew specifies that this number refers to five thousand men, besides women and children (Mt 14:21). If families are no longer an important unit of reckoning in God's sight, Luke would doubtless have counted individual souls in this instance as well.

4. In 1 Corinthians 7:14, the apostle Paul argues that even the children of a family with one believing parent are holy. What does he mean by

holy? Clearly he is not simply stating that they have the privilege of hearing the gospel, for he uses it as an argument to show that the unbelieving spouse is sanctified by the believer. No doubt, Paul is appealing to the fact that the children are covenantally holy on account of their believing parents and, therefore, to be regarded as covenant children. No doubt the Corinthians understood that the children of families with only one believer are covenantally holy, for they were routinely baptised to indicate their status in the covenant.

5. The covenant family remains important under the New Covenant, because both Paul and Peter emphasise the headship of the husband and father, as Moses did. Paul exhorts fathers, in particular, to bring up their children in the nurture and admonition of the Lord (Eph 6:4).

Clearly the place of the family under the New Covenant remains as important as it was under the Old Covenant. It is thus imperative for Christian men and women to know and fulfil their God-ordained roles in the covenant family. They must bring up their covenant children in the fear and nurture of the Lord, appealing to the covenant Lord for the salvation of their children.

Covenant Holiness

The ninth implication of covenant theology is related to the idea of covenant holiness. Biblically, to be holy is to be set apart unto God. Biblically also, there is a sense in which a person or body of people may be regarded as holy on account of the covenant. We think, for example, of how covenant children are holy because they belong to a Christian family (1 Cor 7:14). They may or may not be elect and members of the Covenant of Grace, yet they are regarded as holy because of their relationship with at least one parent who professes to be a member of Christ. Israel was regarded as a holy nation (Ex 19:6) even though a large proportion of her citizens lived and died in unbelief. The nation was holy because she was the flock in which God would nurture the elect members of the Covenant of Grace.

This concept of covenant holiness gives us the warrant to speak to another as a member of Christ even though we cannot see the person's heart and know if he is elect. This same concept allows us to speak of a congregation as holy and belonging to Christ so long as the congregation bears the marks of a true church.[15] These congregations or churches are holy because in them the true members of the Covenant of Grace will ordinarily be found and nurtured.

Covenant Responsibility

The tenth implication of covenant theology is the covenant responsibility of members of the covenant to keep the covenant. This responsibility was most clearly stated in the Moral Law which was revealed in the Mosaic Covenant. That was not the first time that the Moral Law was revealed because man was created in the image of God and, therefore, has the works of the law written in his heart (cf. Rom 2:14–15). But it was the first time that the Law was spoken to God's covenant people and written with the finger of God on tables of stone. The Moral Law, as summarised in the Decalogue, outlines the conditions of the Covenant of Works. Christ kept these conditions on behalf of His elect by perfect obedience while on earth, and also paid the penalty of their violation by dying on the cross for them.

But it must be noted that though Christ kept the Covenant of Works for us, the Covenant of Works was never abrogated. It remains the basis of our covenant relationship with God through Christ, our Mediator. Christ and His Church are one. He is our Covenant Head. His fulfilling the Covenant of Works for us does not imply we are altogether freed from its obligations. No, no; Christ freed us from the curse of the covenant, and secured the promise of the covenant for us, at the same time. He also procured for us the ability to please God

---

[15] "If the pure doctrine of the gospel is preached therein; if it maintains the pure administration of the sacraments as instituted by Christ; if church discipline is exercised in chastening of sin" (*BC* 29).

according to the condition of the covenant. In other words, Christ did not only open the door to heaven, He also made us willing and able to love God in God's appointed way.

To love God is to keep His commandments (1 Jn 5:3). It is thus the responsibility and privilege of God's covenant people, both children and adults, to keep the commandments of God. Children of believers must be taught that they have a covenant responsibility to walk as those who belong to Christ rather than as those who belong to the world.

Covenant Love

The final implication of covenant theology, which we must consider, brings us back to the primary purpose of the covenant. The Covenant of Grace is a bond of love between the Father and Son so that the people represented by the Son may enjoy eternal fellowship with God. The Covenant of Grace is not just a relational framework or merely a mechanism for relationship; it is a bond of love.

We began our studies by noting how a covenant may be well illustrated by marriage. Marriage is more than just a friendship. It is a bond of love undergirded by solemn vows to maintain the relationship. These vows, nevertheless, as it were, fade into insignificance in a marriage that is mutually enjoyed.

As we come to the end of our study, however, we should note that marriage may not be the best illustration of the Covenant of Grace. It serves well when we think of covenants *per se*, but it can be somewhat confusing when applied to the Covenant of Grace. We say this because marriage is cited in Scripture primarily to illustrate the bond of love between Christ and His church (Eph 5:22–23), rather than between the God and His people.

There are, indeed, references in the Old Testament which speak of the relationship between God and His people as a marriage. We think, for example of Ezekiel 16:8:

> *Now when I passed by thee, and looked upon thee, behold, thy time was the time of love; and I spread my skirt over thee, and covered thy nakedness: yea, I sware unto thee, and entered into a covenant with thee, saith the Lord God, and thou becamest mine* (Ezk 16:8).

The reference to marriage is clear. Israel was clearly regarded as the bride of Jehovah. However, we should realise that the focus in this verse is not the *essence* of the Covenant of Grace, but the *administration* of the Covenant of Grace. That becomes clear from the fact that Jehovah would later divorce Israel (the Northern Kingdom) and Judah (the Southern Kingdom), and so break the marriage covenant. The prophet Jeremiah alludes to this divorce in Jeremiah 3:6–10 and 31:32:

- *"The Lord said also unto me in the days of Josiah the king, Hast thou seen that which backsliding Israel hath done? she is gone up upon every high mountain and under every green tree, and there hath played the harlot.[7] And I said after she had done all these things, Turn thou unto me. But she returned not. And her treacherous sister Judah saw it. And I saw, when for all the causes whereby backsliding Israel committed adultery I had put her away, and given her a bill of divorce; yet her treacherous sister Judah feared not, but went and played the harlot also. And it came to pass through the lightness of her whoredom, that she defiled the land, and committed adultery with stones and with stocks. And yet for all this her treacherous sister Judah hath not turned unto me with her whole heart, but feignedly, saith the Lord"* (Jer 3:6–10)

- *"Not according to the covenant that I made with their fathers in the day that I took them by the hand to bring them out of the land of Egypt; which my covenant they brake, although I was an husband unto them, saith the Lord"* (Jer 31:32).

God's marriage covenant with Judah and Israel could be broken; however, the Covenant of Grace cannot be broken. So clearly, marriage was applied to the Old Covenant administration of the Covenant of Grace rather than to the Covenant of Grace itself.

Perhaps a better illustration of the Covenant of Grace would be the relationship between a father and his adopted children. In a way, we are adopted children who were brought home by our Elder Brother, Christ Jesus, who promised to provide for all our needs, to care for us, and to teach us the way of the family of God. It is like an agreement between the Father and the Son with the concurrence of the Holy Spirit. But it is more than that, for the Father and the Son have always enjoyed a relationship of love that goes beyond any agreement or covenant. The covenant is for our sakes. It assures us of the Father's love and the permanence of our relationship with Him. It shows us that nothing shall separate us from His love for it is founded upon the eternal love between the Father and the Son, and made definite by expressed promises.

How should we respond to such a tremendous revelation? Shall we not respond with heartfelt gratitude and love that go beyond keeping the commandments of God? This is why the Holy Spirit is given unto us - for "the love of God is shed abroad in our hearts by the Holy Ghost which is given unto us" (Rom 5:5). The Holy Spirit is the Spirit of Adoption, of whom Paul says: "For ye have not received the spirit of bondage again to fear; but ye have received the Spirit of adoption, whereby we cry, Abba, Father" (Rom 8:15). Let us, therefore, cry "Abba, Father" with hearts overflowing with gratitude for His covenant love towards us and for His provisions by which we who are creatures of dust may enjoy Him forever in a bond that is eternal and unbreakable because it is sealed by the blood of His only begotten Son and by the Spirit indwelling us.

One day we shall enjoy this bond as perfectly as creatures can. In that day, sin will be completely obliterated from us, and our faith and hope will give way to sight. All that remains will be love. We will never forget what Christ has done for us. We will always see God in Christ, for we will always remain creatures. Yet we will be more than creatures, for we shall enjoy such a deep bond of love with the Father as His sons and daughters, that fear, guilt, and even responsibility will find no place in our hearts. All that remains will be love, joy, and peace, world without end. Amen.

13. COVENANT LIFE

Today many professing believers consider the church as merely a place to go for worship on Sunday. Indeed, this attitude is so pervasive that even those who know that church is not just a building often entertain the related notion that church is just a gathering on the Lord's Day. At all other times, the church is dormant or, worst, non-existent. It exists only when it is assembled as a congregation for worship. That has led many into thinking that it is enough just to go to church for worship and then leave. Having fellowship with others in the church is deemed unimportant since church ends with the close of the service. Indeed, some even prefer to go to large churches so they can slip in and out of worship without being noticed. But this pathetic idea of a church makes it no different from a cinema crowd and that is not what the Bible teaches.

The biblical idea of church extends beyond the gathering of a congregation for worship. During the days of the Old Covenant, the church was essentially a covenant community or an extended family that lived, learned, worked, played, and worshipped together. Under the New Covenant, the church is no longer restricted to the family of Israel. But the idea of the church as a covenant community remains. It remains because the church is appointed by God as a means by which God's children may enjoy a loving and fruitful relationship with Him on the basis of the Covenant of Grace. The heart of the church is Christ and all true members of the covenant who are united to Him and therefore to one another.

The apostle Paul likens the church to a body with interdependent members (1 Cor 12:12–26). As a body, the church has a life that goes beyond the Lord's Day and beyond preaching, singing, and listening to the Word of God together. It has a life that involves its members not only in interacting with one another, but in fellowship with and building up one another through the use of the spiritual gifts that the

Lord, the King of the Church has given to them (Eph 4:8; 1 Peter 4:10). Some of these gifts may be exercised on the Lord's Day during worship, while others can only be exercised outside of formal worship. We may describe the life of the church outside formal worship as the covenant life of believers. Every member of the church has a special place in the covenant life of the church.

The covenant life of the church may be distinguished from the worship of the church and the ministry of the Word in that it is not so tightly regulated in the Scriptures. The worship of the church is governed by the principle that whatever is not sanctioned in Scripture is forbidden; and the ministry of the Word, particularly the ministry of preaching, is reserved by the Lord for those whom He has called to be His heralds. On the other hand, the covenant life of the church may be understood as being more broadly regulated in that whatever is not forbidden is allowed with the proviso that: (1) It glorifies God (1 Cor 10:31); (2) it is beneficial (1 Cor 10:23a); (3) it edifies the saints (1 Cor 10:23b); (4) it is not enslaving (1 Cor 6:12b); and (5) it is consistent with biblical examples (1 Cor 11:1).

We may liken regulated worship to the activities appointed to the people within the courtyard of the Old Covenant Tabernacle, whereas covenant life includes all that was permissible and encouraged in the life of the covenant community outside the courtyard of the Tabernacle.

What does the covenant life of the church include? Scripture is relatively silent on this matter. But allow me to suggest several things as we pull together some biblical implications against the background of the doctrine of the covenant and the reality of the covenant community.

Covenant Life
- *Praying for One another*
- *Education of Children*
- *Fellowship Meals*
- *Visitation & Hospitality*
- *Sharing of Possession*
- *Fellowship Meetings*
- *Reformed Cookery 101*

Some of these suggestions may be debatable to some, and others may need to be developed further; but I trust that they will provide a good starting point to think systematically and coherently about how the church should function outside of worship.

Praying for One Another

First and foremost, covenant life would include prayerful concern towards one another. It is sad that in many churches today, very few members know one another, much less are concerned enough to pray for one another. But James reminds us to "pray one for another" (Jas 5:16b). To do so, we must share our burdens with one another (cf. Gal 6:2) and confess our faults (Jas 5:16a). It is sad when members of the church not only fail to pray for each other in private and family worship, but think it is not necessary to join the rest of the church in corporate prayer. It is sadder still when members of the church feel no need to know others in the church and are suspicious of people who try to reach out to them. This ought not to be the case. As members of the church, we must strive to know one another, share our burdens and joys with other, and pray for one another. This will take time and energy. But failing to do so dishonours Christ, who by His blood and Spirit united us into one family as brothers and sisters.

Education of the Children

Second, the covenant life of the church includes educating our children. Yes, the parents of covenant children have the primary responsibility of educating them not only in spiritual things, but also in the things that are needful in this present life (cf. Eph 6:4; Prov 22:6). But the church is a covenant community so we must also help each other in teaching our children. Sabbath classes are one way to do this. In such classes, the church offers catechism classes for the children, led by elders of the church who support the efforts of the children's parents by testing them individually after the parents have taught them at home. We require the elders, and not just any of the brothers, to take this role, although it is not so much a part of the ministry of the Word as it is part of the covenant life of the church because in some ways it is a role that requires authority (over the fathers of the children), and because it is specifically stated in Scripture that elders "must be apt to teach" in the church (1 Tim 3:2). Therefore, in order that all things are done decently and in order, all formal doctrinal instruction in the church should, as far as possible, be assigned to those who have been given the warrant by ordination to instruct, namely the elders and pastors.

But more than the Sabbath class, the Church should really look to either starting a covenant school or supporting our parents to home-school their children. It is quite a sad thing for Christian parents to have to hand over our covenant children to unbelieving teachers and schools to educate them (see 2 Cor 6:14–16). Oh may the Lord grant us the resolve and the resources to meet this vital need of covenant instruction.

Fellowship Meals

Third, seeing that a family that eats together usually stays together, it is recommended that the covenant life of the congregation should include communal meals. The early church practiced what was known as the Agape Meal, usually in conjunction with the Lord's Supper (cf. 1 Cor 11:20–21). Today, a convenient way of fulfilling the same need may be to have members of the church bring their meals to share with one another after worship, or perhaps to have the sisters of the church take turn to cook for the whole congregation upon a rota.

Such fellowship meals encourage the keeping of the Sabbath, as well as provide members of the church with opportunities to catch up with one another in informal settings.

Visitation & Hospitality

Fourth, church members ought to visit each other. Visitation must not be seen as only something for the elders or deacons to do. In the early church, believers regularly had meals in each other's homes. That is what is meant by "breaking bread from house to house" (Acts 2:46). The apostle Peter reminds us to "Use hospitality one to another without grudging" (1 Pet 4:9) and James teaches us that part of pure religion is "to visit the fatherless and widows in their affliction" (Jas 1:27). Hospitality must be part of our covenant life as a church. We should visit those who are suffering affliction to encourage them and pray with them. We should also visit one another to build up our love for each other.

Sharing of Possessions

Fifth, the covenant life of the church might include the mutual exchange of goods and possession. This may sound surprising, but it is really an application of how the early church lived, for we are told, "And all that believed were together, and had all things common; And sold their possessions and goods, and parted them to all men, as every man had need" (Acts 2:44–45). Today, we may not be able to do exactly what the early church did, but surely we can learn to share and exchange things with one another. My family has been given many items for babies such as strollers, clothes, and toys. I am sure most other families with a newborn baby would be glad to be so helped. We can extend this sharing with others things that we no longer need.

Fellowship Meetings

Sixth, the covenant life of the church may include informal meetings of those who share similar interests or concerns in life. Those who live near one another may want to meet regularly to pray with one another or to discuss things that pertain to the kingdom of God. Those who enjoy playing soccer may want to meet together regularly for a game. Our young people may want to gather together to study issues that are of particular concern to them. Of course, such activities must not impinge on the unity of our families or the authority of the church.

I do not believe in having structured groups that are autonomous and might over time become some kind of church within a church. But surely, we may have informal young people's groups that are directly overseen by officers of the church (or even the fathers of some of the young people) as part of the covenant life of the church.

Reformed Cookery 101

Finally, the covenant life of the church should include classes for women taught by women. The apostle Paul sternly admonished: "Let your women keep silence in the churches: for it is not permitted unto them to speak; but they are commanded to be under obedience, as also saith the law" (1 Cor 14:34). He also wrote, "I suffer not a woman to teach, nor to usurp authority over the man, but to be in silence" (1 Tim 2:12). Thus, I do not believe that women should lead a congregation in worship or prayer or Sabbath classes. However, the apostle Paul also instructed Titus to tell the older women to teach the younger women in the church, "to be sober, to love their husbands, to love their children, to be discreet, chaste, keepers at home, good, obedient to their own husbands, that the word of God be not blasphemed" (Tit 2:3–5). Since Paul has already stated that women must not instruct publicly, such as when the church is gathered, what he is referring to here must be the private counsel and admonishment that are part of the covenant life of the church. He advises older women to regard younger women as daughters or younger sisters in the covenant family (cf. 1 Tim 5:2) and to help them as they would their daughters and sisters in the flesh. Unless providence imposes upon them in informal settings such as in the case of the need of Apollos (Acts 18:24-26), they are not to take it upon themselves to instruct in theology. As much as possible, that should be left to the elders and pastors and the husbands of the women (1 Cor 14:35). But they are to teach one another how to be good wives and mothers. As part of the covenant life of the church, older women could lead classes to cultivate skills of mothering, wifery, cooking, and homemaking for younger women, in addition to private counsel.

Conclusion

The church is not just a gathering of people on the Lord's Day. It is a covenant body. Each member is a vital part of this body. Oh may the Lord grant us that with each one of us doing our part, we shall not only grow deeper and deeper in a bond of love with each other, but will in enjoying God through the covenant life of Christ's body, glorify Him. Amen. Ω

Index of Scripture

Selected Bibliography

à Brakel, Wilhelmus. *The Christian's Reasonable Service*. 3 Volumes. Translated by Bartel Elshout. Ligonier: Soli Deo Gloria Publication, 1994.

Belcher, Richard P. *A Comparison of Dispensationalism and Covenant Theology*. Massachusetts: Crowne Publications Inc, 1986.

Berkhof, Louis. *Systematic Theology*. Edinburgh: The Banner of Truth Trust, 1988 (1941).

Boston, Thomas. *A View of the Covenant of Grace From the Sacred Records*. Edingburgh: John Gray, 1775 (reprinted by London: Forgotten Books, 2015)

Confession of Faith and Subordinate Standards of the Free Church of Scotland. Edinburgh: William Blackwood & Sons Ltd, reprinted 1973.

Crenshaw, Curtis I. and Grover E. Gunn, III. *Dispensationalism: Today, Yesterday and Tomorrow*. Memphis, Tennessee: Footstool Publications, 1985.

Golding, Peter. *Covenant Theology: The Key of Theology in Reformed Thought and Tradition*. Ross-shire: Christian Focus Publications, 2004.

Hanko, Herman. *God's Everlasting Covenant of Grace*. Grandville: Reformed Free Publishing Assoc, 1988.

Henry, Matthew. *Matthew Henry's Commentary on the Whole Bible: New Modern Edition* (Peabody: Hendrickson Publishers, 1991

Henry, Matthew. *Matthew Henry's Unpublished Sermons on the Covenant of Grace*. Edited by Allan Harman. Ross-Shire: Christian Focus Publications, 2002.

Hodge, Archibald Alexander. *The Confession of Faith*. Edinburgh: The Banner of Truth Trust, reprinted 1992.

Horton, Michael. *Introducing Covenant Theology*. Grand Rapids: Baker Academic, 2006.

Kline, Meredith. *Treaty of the Great King: The Covenant Structure of Deuteronomy: Studies and Commentary*. Grand Rapids: William B. Erdmans Publishing Company, 1963.

Letham, Robert. *The Westminster Assembly: Reading Its Theology in Historical Context*. Phillipsburg: Presbyterian & Reformed Publishing, 2009.

McKay, David. *The Bond of Love: God's Covenant Relationship with His Church*. Ross-shire: Christian Focus Publications, 2001.

Reymond, Robert. *A New Systematic Theology of the Christian Faith*. Nashville: Thomas Nelson Publishing, 1998.

Robertson, O Palmer. *The Christ of the Covenants*. Phillipsburg, New Jersey: Presbyterian and Reformed Publishing, 1980.

Schenck, Lewis Bevens. *The Presbyterian doctrine of children in the covenant: an historical study of the significance of infant baptism in the Presbyterian Church*. Phillipsburg: Presbyterian & Reformed Publishing, 2002 (1940).

Shaw, Robert. *An Exposition of the Westminster Confession of Faith*. Scotland: Christian Focus Publications, 1992.

Turretin, Francis. *Institutes of Elenctic Theology*. 3 volumes. Translated by George Musgrave Giger. Edited by James T. Dennison, Jr. Phillipsburg: Presbyterian and Reformed Publishing Co., 1994.

Watson, Thomas. *A Body of Divinity*. Edinburgh: The Banner of Truth Trust, 1992 (1692).

Witsius, Herman. *The Economy of the Covenants Between God and Man: Comprehending a Complete Study of Divinity*. 2 Volumes. London: R. Baynes, 1822 (Reprinted Econdido: The den Dulk Christian Foundation, 1990).

Woosley, Andrew A. *Unity and Continuity in Covenantal Thought: A Study in the Reformed Tradition to the Westminster Assembly*. Grand Rapid: Reformation Heritage Book, 2012.

APPENDIX:

AN

INTRODUCTION TO

COVENANT THEOLOGY

(Lecture Notes)

By

JJ Lim

Pilgrim Covenant Church, Singapore
August 2017

All figures referred to are numbered as published in the pages preceding

Lesson #1 Dispensationalism & Its Effects

1. Most Christians know that the Bible mentions "covenants." The Hebrew word that is translated "Covenant" (בְּרִית) occurs 284 times in the Old Testament (eg. Gen 9:9; 17:7; Dt 7:9; Ps 25:14; etc). The Greek word (διαϑήκη) occurs 33 times in the New Testament (eg. Lk 22:20; Heb 12:24; 13:20 etc). But very few know the significance of these words and why they occur all over the Scriptures.

2. The result of this ignorance carries grave consequences for the development of Christian Doctrine, the manner of Christian Life and the functioning of Christian Churches. Arguably, it also has international consequences.

3. Dispensationalism was invented by John Nelson Darby around 1830; popularised by the Scofield Study Bible and DL Moody's campaigns. Today it continues to be promoted by many study bibles; by seminaries such as Dallas Theological Seminary, Masters Seminary, Moody Bible Institute; by theologians such as the late Lewis Sperry Chafer, J. Dwight Pentecost, Charles C Ryrie, John Whitcomb, John MacArthur, etc.

4. Dispensationalism teaches that the Church was not prophesied in the Old Testament. She came into existence as Plan B when the nation of Israel rejected the Messiah. She will be raptured before God deals with Israel again according to the provisions of the Law. After the rapture, Christ will rule the world from a literal throne in Jerusalem for 1000 years, during which time, the Temple will be rebuilt and the sacrificial system will be restored. This millennium will end with the great battle of Gog and Magog (Rev 20:8) before all unbelief is finally conquered and Israel and the Church will enter into the eternal state.

5. Due to Dispensationalism, antinomianism, on the one hand, and legalism, on the other hand, has taken root in the church almost everywhere.

6. Due to Dispensationalism, many Christian are "experts" on what is expected to happen in the last days, but they have very little idea on how they should live today.

7. Due to Dispensationalism, many interpret vast stretches of the Bible as being relevant directly only to Jews and the nation of Israel and only indirectly to Christians and the Church.

8. Due to Dispensationalism, many believe that Israel is still the Holy People of God and the land of Israel is still the holy land to be revered by God's people.

9. Due to Dispensationalism, many churches no longer practice infant baptism.

10. Due in part to Dispensationalism, a kind of Arminianism that emphasises the sinner's prayer for salvation has over taken many churches and parachurch groups.

Lesson #2 Covenant Theology in Broad Strokes

1. Romans 5:12-21 (*Locus classicus* of Covenant Theology) teaches us that God does not only deal with us as individuals, but also as families and federations. I.e., He deals with us covenantally. There are two Covenant Heads: Adam and the Lord Jesus Christ (the second Adam, 1 Cor 15:45). Adam brought sin and death to those he represented; Christ brought righteousness and life to those He represented.

2. Adam represented all mankind descending from him by ordinary generation in the Covenant of Works. Christ represented all the elect in the Covenant of Grace.

3. Covenant of Works:

    a. *Before* the Fall, mankind was also under a covenant relation with God known as the Covenant of Life or the *Covenant of Works*.

    b. WCF 7.2—*"The first covenant made with man was a covenant of works, wherein life was promised to Adam; and in him to his posterity, upon condition of perfect and personal obedience."*

    c. But Adam fell into sin and with him all mankind descending from him by ordinary generation ceased to be able to obtain life by the first covenant.

4. Covenant of Grace:

    a. WCF 7:3—*"Man, by his fall, having made himself incapable of life by that covenant, the Lord was pleased to make a second, commonly called the Covenant of Grace: wherein He freely offereth unto sinners life and salvation by Jesus Christ, requiring of them faith in Him, that they may be saved; and promising to give unto all those that are ordained unto eternal life His Holy Spirit, to make them willing and able to believe."*

    b. WLC 31, Q: *"With whom was the Covenant of Grace made?"* Ans: *"The covenant of grace was made with Christ as the second Adam, and in him with all the elect as his seed."*

    c. Salvation is no longer by works, but by grace through faith in Christ under the Covenant of Grace.

5. Covenant of Works is not the same as the Old Covenant (Heb 8:13). The Old Covenant is the Old Testament administration of the Covenant of Grace, whereas the New Covenant is the New Testament administration of the same Covenant of Grace. There is greater continuity between the Old and New Covenants than between the Covenant of Works and the Covenant of Grace. Salvation is by grace alone through faith alone in Christ alone under both the Old and the New Covenant.

6. Therefore, God has only one people, not two. Under the Old Testament, God's people were mostly Jewish or in the nation of Israel (after Jacob); whereas under the New Testament, God's people is mostly Gentile and are found in the Church Visible.

7. Therefore, it is not quite right to say that Christians are under grace while the Jews (or Israelites) were under the Law. The Moral Law (as summarised in the Ten Commandments) are not only for the Jews, but for Christians and indeed for all men. The Ceremonial Law is not applicable to New Testament Christians only because it is fulfilled in Christ. The Civil Law is not directly applicable to New Testament Christians only because the covenant people of God is no longer gathered as a nation in a specific locality.

8. Therefore, many Old Testament prophecies about Judah and Israel is really about God's Covenant People, which is the Church in the New Testament (Israel being the church-underage in the Old Testament).

9. Therefore, there is an essential (of the essence) continuity between the sacraments of the Old Testament and those of the New Testament. This is one reason why we baptise our children today.

10. Therefore, although many Reformed Theologians expect a mass conversion of the Jews towards the Last Day, we should not think of General Eschatology as being centred on the nation of Israel. In fact, it is unlikely that the re-gathering of Israel in 1948 is a fulfilment of Isaiah 11:11 or 60:9; nor should we think that God's promise to Abraham in Gen 15:18-21 has not been fulfilled (cf. Jos 21:43-45; 1 Kgs 4:21, 24).

Lesson #3 Covenants in the Bible

1. Covenants are like contracts. The Old Testament word translated "Covenant" (בְּרִית) is used to describe bi-lateral agreements between man and man, eg. between Abraham and Abimelech, (Gen 21:32); between Isaac and the later Abimelech (Gen 26:28); between Jacob and Laban (Gen 31:44); between Israel

and the Gibeonites (Jos 9:15); and between King Solomon and King Hiram of Tyre (1 Kgs 5:12).

2. These covenants involve: (1) Two parties; (2) a set of conditions; (3) Blessings for fulfilling the conditions; (4) Curses for failing to keep the conditions. They usually also include witnesses (apart from God), and a pledge or sign and seal,[16] though these are not of the essence of the covenant and are therefore optional.

3. Some of these covenants are purely transactional and tend to emphasise the penalty of failing to keep the promises made (e.g. Gen 31:44). Others involve a relationship of friendship or love. The covenants between Israel and Gibeon, and Solomon and Hiram are like that (1 Kgs 5:12).

4. God's Covenant with man is like the second kind. It may be defined as a bond of friendship or love that is sealed by promissory oaths. It's like marriage: More than a mere contract, and more than a friendship; but rather, a bond of love sealed by promissory oaths.

5. But God is infinitely greater than man. It cannot be that God has made an agreement with man as if God and man were equal parties in the covenant; for God is sovereign and in control of all things whereas man is a finite creature. Therefore the terms of any covenant between God and Man can only be dictated by God. And especially after the Fall, it is impossible for man to keep any condition stipulated by God; therefore, in a sense, post-Fall, God alone must keep the covenant for both parties.

6. Genesis 15 illustrates with God's covenant with Abraham (v. 18). This was validated according to the ancient Near-Eastern customs of covenant-making, in which several animals were cut in half and laid out so both parties of the covenant could walk between the pieces while calling a curse upon themselves if they failed to keep their promise (cf. Jer. 34:18). Abraham did not pass through the pieces; he was fast asleep though he was made aware of what was going on (v. 12). What passed through the pieces was clearly a theophany (v. 17).

7. For this reason, and the reason that the New Testament translates בְּרִית with διαθήκη (which is often translated in the English New Testament as

---

[16] In the covenant between Abraham and Abimelech, the pledge was "seven ewe lambs" (Gen 21:30) whereas in the covenant between Jacob and Laban, the pledge or witness was a heap of stone (Gen 31:48).

"Testament" i.e. "will", eg. Heb 9:16-17), rather than συνθήκη (which clearly carries the idea of a bi-lateral compact), many commentators insist that God's Covenant with man must never be viewed as conditional bilateral, but as unconditional and unilateral.

8. But the problem is that συνθήκη occurs very rarely in the LXX (Dan 11:6; Isa 28:15; 30:1; and apocrypha: Wis 1:16; 1 Mac 10:26) and is used to translate בְּרִית only once;[17] whereas διαθήκη is also used to translate בְּרִית when it refers to conditional, bilateral covenants between man and man (eg. Gen 21:27, 32; 26:28; 31:44 etc). Thus διαθήκη does not necessarily imply unilateral unconditional covenant.

9. So we can't run away from the idea that biblical covenants, whether human or divine, do involve some form of bilateral agreement. Therefore, the idea that God relates to man by way of covenant simply because the persons in the Godhead enjoy an ontological covenant relationship (which is necessarily unconditional) does not have strong biblical basis.[18]

10. A better way to understand the need for covenants is to see it as the framework that God has chosen to enable finite men to understand and enjoy their relationship with Him. Thus, *WCF* 7.1—"*The distance between God and the creature is so great, that although reasonable creatures do owe obedience unto Him as their Creator, yet they could never have any fruition of Him as their blessedness and reward, but by some voluntary condescension on God's part, which He hath been pleased to express by way of covenant.*"[19]

Lesson #4 Covenant of Works

1. The *Westminster Confession of Faith*, having explained the necessity of the covenant as a relational framework to bridge the distance between infinite God and finite man, proceeds immediately to show us how it actually works out:

---

[17] Possibly because διαθήκη is already used in the same statement, or perhaps because of a translational error, for the Hebrew may better be rendered, " Ὅτι εἴπατε Ἐποιήσαμεν διαθήκην μετὰ τοῦ θανάτου καὶ μετὰ τοῦ ἅδου συνθήκας..." than "Ὅτι εἴπατε Ἐποιήσαμεν διαθήκην μετὰ τοῦ ἅδου καὶ μετὰ τοῦ θανάτου συνθήκας..."

[18] This same idea has led some to deny the Covenant of Works, which is why we need to address it.

[19] With full assent to what we are given to confess, we do not believe that we should appeal to the Ancient Near Eastern/Ugaritic/Hittite Royal Grant or Suzerainty Treaty approach of Meredith Kline, Michael Horton and others to explain the Covenant of Works or the Covenant of Grace. We believe, rather that these covenants eventually came about because God first introduced the idea of covenant to mankind.

WCF 7.2—"The first covenant made with man was a Covenant of Works, wherein life was promised to Adam; and in him to his posterity upon condition of perfect and personal obedience."

2. The first man, Adam, was the appointed representative of man. God would deal with Adam as the head of the federation of mankind. Adam's role in the covenant would be like the role of a king in entering into a covenant relationship with another nation. If the king breaks the covenant, every citizen of his nation breaks the covenant. If the king declares war, every citizen in his nation is at war. See Figure 6.

3. The covenant that God made with Adam is known as the Covenant of Works, or the Covenant of Life. It is called the Covenant of Life because the blessing of the covenant was life, whereas its penalty was death. It is called the Covenant of Works because the condition stipulated by God for man to enjoy life is perfect and personal obedience of God's Law. See Figure 7.

4. In the administration of the covenant, God instructed Adam not to eat of a special tree in the Garden of Eden known as the Tree of the Knowledge of Good and Evil. God told Adam: "Thou shalt not eat of it: for in the day that thou eatest thereof thou shalt surely die" (Gen. 2:17). This was a test of obedience for Adam. Adam must not eat of the tree not because the fruit could be poisonous, but because God forbade him from doing so. If he ate from the tree, he would violate the condition of the covenant, which is perfect, perpetual, personal obedience to God, and die.

5. Some object that the word "covenant" does not appear in Genesis 1 to 3 and, therefore, it is unbiblical to speak of a Covenant of Works. However, apart from the fact that the elements of a covenant are implied in God's interaction with Adam, there are three other good reasons to believe that God did make a covenant with Adam:

6. First, the Hebrew of Hosea 6:7 is rightly rendered: "They like Adam have transgressed the covenant" (cf. Job 31:33) rather than "They like men have transgressed the covenant."

7. Second, the apostle Paul offers a clear parallel between Adam and Christ in Romans 5:12–21 in connection with the doctrine of justification. This parallel can only make sense if Adam, like Christ, is the representative of a covenant. Just as Adam's sin was imputed to his posterity whom he represented, Christ's righteousness is imputed to the elect whom He represents.

8. Third, the gospels include a couple of occasions when the Lord Jesus is asked: "What shall I do that I may inherit eternal life?" (Mk 10:17; cf Mt 19:16; Lk 18:18; see also Lk 10:25). In each instance, the Lord's answer is, essentially, to keep the law perfectly. Is the Lord wrong or deceitful in His answer? Of course not! But surely, He is not suggesting that law-keeping or good works can merit eternal life. Even in man's unfallen state in the Garden of Eden, obedience was his expected duty, not something that merited anything (Luke 17:10). The fact is: if there were no Covenant of Works, obedience could not obtain eternal life. So our Lord's answer only makes sense if there is indeed a Covenant of Works, which has not been abrogated. If there were no Covenant of Works or it was abrogated, then the Lord's answer would be erroneous or deceitful, which would contradict His divine nature. The inquirers had asked what they could do to obtain eternal life. The Lord honestly answered that the only way of obtaining life by *doing* is through perfect obedience of God's law under the provision of the Covenant of Works (cf. Rom 7:10; 10:5; Lev 18:5; Gal 3:12, etc)! Of course, fallen man cannot keep the Covenant of Works. Fallen man may only obtain life by faith in the One who kept the Covenant of Works, even Jesus!

9. The *quality* of eternal life that could be obtained by Adam's obedience could not possibly have been nearly as complete as what is obtained by Christ's obedience, for Adam was created as a man whereas Christ is the God-Man. But we have scriptural warrant to speak of the benefit of the Covenant of Works as being eternal life. In a sense, Adam was already enjoying a degree of eternal life before the Fall, for eternal life according to the Lord Jesus is a life of knowing and enjoying God. That is what He is essentially saying in His high priestly prayer: "This is life eternal, that they might know thee the only true God, and Jesus Christ, whom thou hast sent" (Jn 17:3).

10. As it turns out, Adam ate the forbidden fruit. Thus, he broke the covenant, and all his descendants by ordinary generation became covenant-breakers and are liable for the penalty of the covenant. God never revoked the Covenant of Works, but we can never again have life by the Covenant of Works because we are by nature guilty in Adam. We are saved today not through the Covenant of Works, but through Christ's work as the Mediator of the Covenant of Grace.

Lesson #5 Significance of the Covenant of Works

1. The doctrine of the Covenant of Life is important, first of all, for us to understand that God intends for man to enjoy His friendship. When we enjoy someone's friendship, we derive pleasure from giving to and receiving from that

person. But man is a creature of dust. How could we enjoy fellowship with the almighty God? Why should God give in response to our giving? He owes us nothing. This is the reason why he entered into a Covenant of Life with us: that we may know he did not intend our relationship with him to be merely that between Creator and Creature.

2. Secondly, the Covenant of Life is a wonderful display of God's wisdom. It is not an end in itself; it is rather a means to an end. God never intended for the elect to obtain eternal life through Adam's obedience. Christ was always in the plan of salvation. He was never a secondary option. God in His wisdom set the Covenant of Life in place, first, as a stepping stone to the Covenant of Grace, and second, to demonstrate His fairness and wisdom.

3. Thirdly, the Covenant of Life provides us with a vivid demonstration of God's grace. God's eternal plan is that a multitude of sons and daughters share His image to enjoy fellowship with Him for all eternity with a personal knowledge of the fullness of His mercy and justice. He could have created us in an instant the way that He created angels. He could also have made us infallibly righteous. But He preferred to have us know Him as a just God who is full of mercy and grace. This is why He created man with the capacity to disobey. That is also why He ordained the Covenant of Life, for it helps man realize that he cannot obtain life by himself even though God promises to reward him with life if he chooses to love and obey Him. The covenant provided the way to have life, but man forfeited the right. Man deserves to be cast away forever, yet God graciously brought man to Himself.

4. Fourthly, an understanding of the doctrine of the Covenant of Works or Covenant of Life is necessary for a proper exegesis of those passages where the Lord Jesus asserts that one may obtain eternal life by the keeping of God's commandment.

5. Fifthly, it provides us with a theological framework for interpreting the work of the Lord Jesus Christ, particularly in His Active (or Preceptive) and Passive (or Punitive) Obedience on behalf of the elect.[20]

---

[20] Without Covenant of Works, we are essentially left with no theological basis to explain Active Obedience. While it is true that Passive Obedience may be explained by an appeal to the justice of God, the Covenant of Works gives us a more complete and systematic basis to expound it since it explains the covenant representation of Adam and the guilt of all descending from him by natural generation.

6. Sixthly, the sad state that the world is in today is in fact a result of the implementation of the curses threatened to Adam in the Covenant of Works. The LORD had warned Adam: "But of the tree of the knowledge of good and evil, thou shalt not eat of it: for in the day that thou eatest thereof *thou shalt surely die*" (Gen 2:17). The intensity of the words in Hebrew (תָּמוּת מוֹת: "dying, ye shall die") suggests that more than physical death is involved. Comparing Scripture with Scripture, we may conclude that three levels of death are involved: physical, spiritual, and eternal (cf. *WCF* 6.6).

7. *Physical death* refers to bodily degradation and demise. The minute Adam violated the covenant, his body, in a sense, died, for he could no longer glorify or enjoy God with his body. And moreover, he became mortal. He began the process of bodily decay which would eventually lead to death.

8. *Spiritual death* refers to deadness in the soul, making a person totally unable to do good in the sight of God or to glorify and enjoy God. When Adam fell, he and his posterity became "dead in trespasses and sin" (Eph 2:1), and all their righteousness were as "filthy rags" (Isa 64:6) in the eyes of God.

9. *Eternal death* refers to the permanent inability to enjoy God's fellowship and love in this life, which inevitably culminates at bodily death, to suffering the full wrath of God forever and ever. Eternal death is symbolized in Genesis 3:24 when the Lord drives Adam out of the Garden of Eden.

10. Seventhly, the Covenant of Life or Covenant of Works provides the proper basis for understanding the Covenant of Grace.

Lesson #6 Covenant of Grace

1. God graciously covenanted to reward Adam and his posterity with life upon condition of perfect personal obedience. But Adam fell into sin, and with him, all mankind descending from him by ordinary generation could no longer obtain life by the first covenant.

2. The Covenant of Grace is God's gracious provision for fallen man to enjoy life. This covenant is not an afterthought which God instituted only after the Covenant of Works failed. It has always been in God's mind and logically precedes the Covenant of Works, which is, as it were, a stepping stone to it.

3. The Covenant of Grace is referred to in numerous places in Scripture, but Genesis 15 provides us with, perhaps, the most complete and beautiful picture

of it. Here we see God encouraging Abram by reiterating His covenant promise to him that he would have many children and would inherit the Promised Land (v. 13, 18), which promise would be fulfilled literally and spiritually (cf. 1 Kgs 4:21–24; Lk 1:67–75). But what is most striking is that He instructed Abram to prepare for a covenant-cutting ceremony (cf. Jer 34:18-19), but did not require Abram to pass through the animal pieces. He himself passed through the pieces in two theophanies that most likely represented the Father (cf. Mt 13:42) and the Son (Jn 1:9)[21] that by two immutable things (the theophanies) we "might have a strong consolation, who have fled for refuge to lay hold upon the hope set before us" (Heb 6:13–18).

4. Christ came to fulfil the Covenant of Works on behalf of His elect, and also pay for their penalty due to their violation of the Covenant of Works in Adam and in themselves (cf. 1 Cor 15:20-21). See Figure 9.

5. While the human party of the Covenant of Works is Adam and all his posterity descending from him by natural generation, the human party of the Covenant of Grace is Christ and all the elect, or in other words, the Church Invisible Universal. Since man cannot consciously relate to the Church Invisible as an entity, God appointed the Church Visible to serve as the earthly manifestation and nursery of the Church Invisible. So we speak of Israel of the Old Testament (the Church Under-Age) and the Church Visible in the New Testament as the covenant people of God under the Covenant of Grace, or more precisely, under the administration of the Covenant of Grace. But only the true members of the Covenant of Grace will be given faith by the Holy Spirit and therefore enabled truly to enjoy the blessings of the covenant. See Figure 8.

6. Such is the close relationship between the Church Visible and the Church Invisible that we may tabulate it. See Figure 13.

7. Similarly, the ordinary progression of a member of the covenant may be seen in Figure 14.

8. *Question*: Is faith a condition of the Covenant of Grace (cf. *WLC* 32)? *Answer*: No; Christ fulfilled the condition of the Covenant of Grace, but faith is appointed as the instrument by which the members of the Covenant may enjoy the blessings of the Covenant procured by Christ. *WLC* 32 speaks of faith as an instrumental rather than meritorious condition.

---

[21] See (JJ Lim, *Covenant Theology: A Primer* [Singapore: Pilgrim Covenant Church, 2019], 32-33).

9. *Question*: If Christ kept the condition of the Covenant of Grace perfectly, do members of the Covenant of Grace have any covenant responsibility apart from faith in Christ? *Answer*: Yes, for the Covenant of Works was never annulled. Christ not only fulfilled the Covenant of Works for us (so as to remove its curse, and purchase its blessing), but also enabled us personally to keep the condition of the Covenant of Works by genuine love and gratitude. This is why the Ten Commandments is known as the "words of the Covenant" (Ex 34:27). Additionally, all members of the Covenant have the responsibility to walk according to the administrative provisions of the Covenant by making use of the means of grace.

10. *Question*: If Christ fulfilled the Covenant of Grace perfectly, can anyone be said to be a covenant-breaker under the Covenant of Grace? *Answer*: Not formally and finally; but practically, (1) one who does not walk according to the "Words of the Covenant" or according to administrative provisions of the Covenant is breaking the covenant; and (2) one who is a external member of the Covenant (i.e. a member of the Church Visible) who has been excommunicated or who dies in unbelief may be regarded as a covenant-breaker.

Lesson #7 Covenant of Grace in Redemptive History (OT)

1. The "Covenant of Grace" may be said to be a theological rather than a biblical term since it cannot be found directly in the Bible. However, it is a reality that actually undergirds all of God's dealings with His people through the ages, and therefore is alluded to and used theologically everywhere in the Scripture.

2. *WCF 7.5*—This covenant [i.e. the Covenant of Grace] was differently administered in the time of the law, and in the time of the gospel: under the law it was administered by promises, prophecies, sacrifices, circumcision, the paschal lamb, and other types and ordinances delivered to the people of the Jews, all fore-signifying Christ to come; which were, for that time, sufficient and efficacious, through the operation of the Spirit, to instruct and build up the elect in faith in the promised Messiah, by whom they had full remission of sins, and eternal salvation; and is called the Old Testament.

3. *WCF 7.6*—Under the gospel, when Christ, the substance, was exhibited, the ordinances in which this covenant is dispensed are the preaching of the Word, and the administration of the sacraments of Baptism and the Lord's Supper: which, though fewer in number, and administered with more simplicity and less outward glory, yet, in them, it is held forth in more fullness, evidence, and spiritual efficacy, to all nations, both Jews and Gentiles; and is called the New

Testament. There are not therefore two covenants of grace differing in substance, but one and the same under various dispensations

4. There is only one Covenant of Grace which was administered differently in the Old and New Testaments. This is clear from the fact that: (1) Christ is the Saviour of men before and after His advent (see Rev 13:8; Rom 3:25; Heb 9:15; Col 2:17; Heb 10:1-10 etc); and (2) Faith in Christ was the instrumental cause of salvation in the Old and New Testaments: "the just shall live by his faith" (Hab 2:4; cf. Ps 2:12; Rom 1:17; Gal 3:11; Heb 10:38; Heb 11; etc).

5. Reading the Scriptures, one cannot fail to see that there are various covenants between God and His people mentioned in the inspired records of the historical progress of the Church underage in the Old Testament. A careful study of these covenants reveals that they are all historical administrations of the one Covenant of Grace! We may say that these historical covenants are really subordinate covenants of the Covenant of Grace. In themselves, these subordinate covenants may not even appear to take the form of a covenant, though careful reflection will show that they in fact visible imprints of the Covenant of Grace in history with Christ and His visible body on the human side of the covenant. We may also think of the Covenant of Grace as a man walking through history, and each of the subordinate covenants as an outer jacket worn by the man. One by one, these jackets are shed until the New Covenant is revealed.

6. There are five Old Testament subordinate covenants (see Figure 10):

    a. The Adamic Covenant, under which the Messiah was first promised, and bloody sacrifices were introduced to point to the Messiah (see Gen 3:15, 21; 4:1-4).

    b. The Noahic Covenant, under which God announces the religious significance of blood for atonement and therefore the prohibition of eating blood (Cf. Gen. 9:4; Lev 17:11) to clarify that salvation must be procured by the propitiatory death of the Messiah. Under which also God's people are given the sign of the rainbow (Gen 9:13) to assure them that the world will be preserved until Messiah comes.

    c. The Abrahamic Covenant, under which not only is the Covenant of Grace symbolically dramatised, but the sacrament of circumcision as a sign and seal of the covenant is introduced to mark out God's covenant people (cf. Gen 12, 15).

d. The Mosaic Covenant, under which the Ceremonial Law is set in place (Ex 24–30) to instruct God's people about the theology of the atonement, and to prepare them for the atoning work of the Messiah (Ex 24-30). At the same time, the Moral Law (Ex 19–20), which is a way of life for God's people, is summarized and codified.[22]

e. The Davidic Covenant, which makes the kingship of Christ obvious (cf. 2 Sam 7:12–13).

8. We can see a *thematic* unity between these subordinate covenants in that under each administration God declares something to the effect, "I shall be your God; you shall be my people" (cf. Gen 3:15; 9:9; 17:7; Ex 6:6-7; Lev 26:12; 2 Sam 7:24).

9. We can see a *structural* unity in that each administration appears to build upon the previous ones (eg. Ex 6:3-8; 1 Kgs 2:3; Ezk 37:24-27).

10. Unless we understand that all these covenants are administrations or divine provisions appointed by God for His people to relate to Him on the basis of the gracious eternal covenant, we will misinterpret Scripture and read a legalistic religion into Scripture which sidelines Christ.

Lesson #8 Covenant of Grace in Redemptive History (NT)

1. The divine covenants of the Old Testament are subordinates of the Covenant of Grace which are administered with different emphases to God's people living in different ages and related to one another by structure and theme.

2. The New Covenant is also a subordinate covenant which is structurally and thematically united to the Old Testament subordinate covenants. *Structurally*, we see, for example, how the apostle Peter refers to the promise of the Abrahamic Covenant to instruct the inaugural new covenant congregation about repentance and baptism (Acts 2:38–39; Gal 3:13-14). *Thematically*, we see, for example, how Paul appeals to the theme of the Old Covenant as stated under the Mosaic Covenant (see Lev. 26:12) to urge the New Testament saints to live holy lives, separate from the world (see 2 Cor 6:14-16).

---

[22] We may use the term "republished" but unlike Meredith Kline and Michael Horton, we do not believe that the Covenant of Works is republish. Only the Moral Law given at creation is republished, obviously in its post-lapsarian form.

3. The Covenant of Grace is administered in the New Covenant in greater simplicity, clearness and fullness since Christ, the Anti-type (of the Old Covenant types), has completed His work of redemption.

4. The New Covenant is superior to the Old Covenant (encompassing all the subordinate covenants of the Old Testament) for the following reasons:

   a. It is administered by Christ the Son, rather than servants such as Moses (cf. Heb 3:5–6).

   b. Before, the truth was partly hidden, partly revealed in types and symbols, but now it is revealed in the clear history of the Incarnation together with the inspired commentaries of the apostles.

   c. The old administration was largely external, carnal, and ceremonial and involved land, temples, sacrifices, rituals, and feasts. But under the New Covenant, the administration becomes largely internal and spiritual, apart from the two sacraments, Baptism and the Lord's Supper.

   d. The bloody signs and seals of the covenant under the Old Covenant administration, namely, Circumcision and the Passover have been replaced with the bloodless sacraments of Baptism and the Lord's Supper.

   e. Membership in the covenant had been largely confined to one people, but now it embraces people from the whole world without racial or geographic distinction.

   f. The Old Covenant emphasised an external law and motivates by threats. The New Covenant involves internalisation of the Law through regeneration and indwelling of the Holy Spirit (Jer. 31:33; cf. Ezek 11:19), and motivates by love and gratitude.

   g. Under the Old Covenant, the work of the Holy Spirit in regeneration, illumination and sanctification was comparatively limited in extent and degree; whereas under the New Covenant, the Spirit has, as it were, been poured out so that many more of God's people are recipients of His grace and that, in a more intense measure.

5. Understanding Covenant Theology, we know that it is not only an error to say that Old Testament saints were saved by obedience whereas New Testament saints are saved by faith; it is also an error to think that Old Testament saints did not have the Spirit indwelling them or that they did not experience the benefits of salvation that New Testament Saints enjoy. That is not to say that there is no qualitative and quantitative difference as Figure 11 illustrates.

6. *Question*: Why does *WSC* 92 speak of sacraments as ordinances that represent, seal and apply to believers "the benefits of the <u>New</u> Covenant"? *Answer*: The New Covenant is not only one of the administrations of the Covenant of Grace; it is the final administration before the eternal state, and it is under this administration that Christ and His work is revealed in clear.

7. *Question*: Is it right to say that the Holy Spirit worked *upon* the heart of Old Testament saints, but *in* the heart of New Testament saints. *Answer*: No, that is not right for the Old and New Covenant do not differ in essence. However, it is true that a larger percentage of the Old Testament people of God were not true believers (Heb 3:18-4:2) and so enjoyed only the external operations of the Holy Spirit.

8. Dispensationalists understand the Bible to be organized into seven dispensations: Innocence (Gen 1:1-3:7), Conscience (Gen 3:8-8:22), Human Government (Gen 9:1-11:32), Promise (Gen 12:1-Ex 19:25), Law (Ex 20:1-Acts 2:4), Grace (Acts 2:4-Rev 20:3), and the Millennial Kingdom (Rev 20:4-6). In Dispensationalism God deals with His people according to a pattern that include (1) a responsibility, (2) a failure, (3) a judgment, and (4) grace to move on. Some believe that the responsibility is tied to salvation, some do not.

9. This scheme of interpreting the history of redemption is very different from the manner adopted by Covenant Theologians which recognises the Covenant of Works followed by six subordinate covenants (of Grace): Adamic, Noahic, Abrahamic, Mosaic, Davidic and New Covenant, followed by the eternal state.

10. They are very different, for the Dispensational scheme emphasises discontinuity and human effort whereas the Covenant scheme emphasises continuity and God's work of redemption under an overarching plan which sees all the subordinate covenants or administration of the eternal Covenant of Grace related thematically and structurally with one another.

Lesson #9 Implications of Covenant Theology

1. Covenant Salvation: If Covenant Theology as presented is the truth, then fallen man can only be saved by grace alone, through faith alone in Christ alone (regardless of whether they live under the Old Testament or the New Testament) since all men descending from Adam by natural generation are guilty in Him and therefore cannot fulfil the condition for salvation in the Covenant of Works.

2. Covenant People: If there is only one Covenant of Grace and both the Old Covenant and the New Covenant are subordinate to it, it follows that the saints of the Old and New Covenant are one. God does not regard Israel as a distinct people and the church as another distinct people. The Visible Church is likened to an Olive Tree by the apostle Paul in Romans 11. This Olive Tree was more Jewish in Old Testament days, but became more Gentile after the Jews who rejected Christ and the New Covenant were cut off.

3. Covenant Worship: The third implication of the doctrine of the Covenant is that our worship must be covenantal. If our relationship to God is covenantal at heart, and is mediated by Christ our covenant Head, then surely our worship must be covenantal and mediated by Christ. Thus, the right question to ask when deciding how we should worship is not what is popular, but what Christ appointed and how Christ would worship as the Worshipper-in-Chief.

4. Covenant Life: Since God has appointed the Church Visible to serve as the earthly manifestation and nursery of the Church Invisible or the covenant body of Christ, it is essential that all local manifestations of the Church Visible function covenantally. Remember how Scripture speaks of those who are members of the Visible Church as members of the Covenant. Therefore it is appropriate that members of the Church Local relate to one another as family members with Christ as our elder brother; and it is also appropriate for the Church to make use of Church Covenant by which members bind themselves more strictly to serve the Lord together as the body of Christ (eg. 2 Chr 15:12; 2 Kgs 23:3; Neh 9:38). See Figure 12.

5. Covenant Sabbath: The fifth implication of the doctrine of the covenant is that God's people should keep the Sabbath as a covenant sign which identifies them as God's people (see Ex 31:13–17; cf. Heb 4:9).

6. Covenant Membership: Since circumcision was appointed by God to serve as the sign and seal to mark His external covenant people in the Old Covenant, and since baptism has replaced circumcision (Col 2:11-12), it is appropriate that covenant infants today be baptised. We baptise them because they are members of the covenant seeing they grew on the Olive Tree. We do not baptise them to make them members.

7. Covenant Family: From Adam to Noah to Abraham to Jacob, it is clear that the family and familial descend is intrinsic to the outworking of God's promises in the Covenant of Grace in the Old Covenant. From the words of the apostle

Peter at Pentecost (Acts 2:39); the references to household baptism; Paul's assertion of holiness by family connection (1 Cor 7:14), etc, it is clear that the covenant family remains intrinsic to the outworking of God's promises under the New Covenant. The Lord remains pleased to use Christian families as the primary nursery for true members of the covenant (ie. the elect) to be brought unto salvation. Covenant Parents must bring up their children in the fear and nurture of the Lord, appealing to the covenant Lord for the salvation of their children.

8. Covenant Holiness: Because of the inalienable connection between the Church Visible (the external covenant people of God) and the Church Invisible (the eternal covenant people of God), the Church Visible is holy in God's eyes, and individual members of the Church Visible including children are to be regarded and treated as holy and belonging to Christ (cf. Ex 19:6; 1 Cor 7:14).

9. Covenant Responsibility: Although the Covenant of Grace is fulfilled by Christ and is therefore enjoyed unconditionally for those He represented, it is essential for all His members to make use of the means of grace that is appointed by the Lord under each subordinate covenant administration. Moreover, Christ not only fulfilled the Covenant of Works for us (so as to remove its curse, and purchase its blessing), but also enabled us personally to keep the condition of the Covenant of Works by genuine love and gratitude. Therefore, it is the responsibility and privilege of God's covenant people, both children and adults, to keep the commandments of God.

10. Covenant Love: Marriage is used in Scripture primarily to illustrate the bond of love between Christ and His church (Eph. 5:22–23), as well as the relationship between God and His covenant people according to the administration rather than the essence of the Covenant of Grace. This relationship can be broken (cf. Jer 3:6-10; 31:32). A better illustration of the Covenant of Grace would be the relationship between a father and his adopted children. We are adopted children who were brought home by our Elder Brother, Christ Jesus, who promised to provide for all our needs, to care for us, and to teach us the way of the family of God. This relationship can never be broken. It is a relation in which duties and responsibilities increasingly gives way to love until love alone remains (1 Cor 13:13). Therefore the Christian ministry must emphasis love together with faith and hope rather than duties and chastisement.

Lesson #10

TEST!

Contact author at jjlim.pcc@gmail.com

77503372R00069